BoB ☑ W9-APK-546

Praise for "WAKE-UP CALLS"

"A celebration of our own potential for limitless growth. It will help many to awaken."

Dr. Wayne W. Dyer
Author of *You'll See It When You Believe It* and *Real Magic*

"A fantastic book! Magical—compelling. A refreshing, gentle invitation to become far more than you ever imagined. It makes it safe and easy to grow."

Ann McGee-Cooper, Ed.D.
Author of *You Don't Have to Go Home from Work Exhausted!*

"A beautiful book. *Wake-Up Calls* is full of practical ways to enhance your personal growth."

Ken Keyes, Jr.
Author of *Handbook to Higher Consciousness*

"*Wake-Up Calls* is a must for today's leadership reading. Eric has placed in writing the principles that have revolutionized the leadership team at my hospital."

Jim Boyle, President/CEO
Shawnee Mission Medical Center

"This wonderful book is full of ideas and insights that constantly alert you to your possibilities and potentialities. It will take you on a journey of increased inner awareness and outer effectiveness. You may never be the same again."

Brian Tracy
Brian Tracy Learning Systems

"*Wake-Up Calls* is a clear, imaginative, and resourceful manual filled with vision, wisdom, and integrity. This masterful synthesis of insight and heart will be a welcome asset to anyone seeking to further their personal and professional growth."

Alan Cohen
Author of *The Dragon Doesn't Live Here Anymore*

"This book will assist people and businesses to learn, grow, and succeed. There is something here for everyone. Keep it on your bedstand next to your alarm clock and discover your own 'wake-up calls.'"

Gary V. Koyen, Ph.D.
The Meridian Institute, Inc.

"*Wake-Up Calls* takes the reader to a new octave of personal and professional growth. With wit, wisdom, and easily usable tools, Dr. Allenbaugh shows how to turn life's challenges into life's greatest opportunities."

Mary Manin Boggs, Minister/CEO
Living Enrichment Center

"*Wake-Up Calls* is a winner! Recognizing breakthrough moments becomes a stepping-stone to further discovery. A masterful job of combining wit and wisdom to further assist this process. The quotes alone are worth the price of the book."

Earnie Larsen
Author of *Old Patterns, New Truths*

"I loved it! Thank you for the research, thank you for the passion, and thank you for listening to your wake-up calls to get this important work completed."

Bob Moawad, Chairman/CEO
Edge Learning Institute

Eric Allenbaugh, Ph.D.

WAKE-UP CALLS

You Don't Have to Sleepwalk Through Your Life, Love, or Career!

Eric Allenbaugh, Ph.D.

DISCOVERY PUBLICATIONS

A BARD PRESS BOOK

For more information about quantity discounts, call:

Bard Press
An imprint of Longstreet Press
800-945-3132

ISBN 0-9631194-1-9

Fifth printing: July 2000

A BARD PRESS BOOK
AUSTIN, TEXAS

Copyediting: **Helen Hyams**
Text Design: **Suzanne Pustejovsky**
Jacket Design: **Suzanne Pustejovsky**
Composition/Production: **Round Rock Graphics**
Indexing: **Linda Webster**

To the memory of my Dad,

whose love of life

and positive energy

continues to serve as

an inspiration.

TABLE OF CONTENTS

ACKNOWLEDGMENTS

M any people have contributed to the creation of this book through their loving influence. Kay, my wife, supported and encouraged me from the very beginning. Her unconditional love, while it was genuinely appreciated in the development of this book, is even more significant in the context of the joy and fulfillment of our shared life experience. Our journey is loving, fun, spiritual, and empowering. Thank you, Kay.

Some other life teachers have assisted me in punching through important barriers and experiencing life at a more complete level. Gary Koyen, James Newton, and Will Schutz have each had a profound influence on my personal growth in recent years. Glenn Grab, Richard Stevens, and Herman Adams, important life teachers in high school "centuries" ago, continue to share a positive place in my memories of growth experiences.

Mom and Dad, significant forces in my life, served as positive role models for both parenting and loving relationships. Our boys have also been important teachers in my life experiences. The Reverend Mary Manin Boggs continues to be a friend and inspiration in my spiritual journey.

Ray Bard, my book producer, has treated this project with professional, yet caring, commitment. Friends and clients, too numerous to name individually, have also been sources of learning, support, and inspiration in my life's journey—and in the writing of *Wake-Up Calls*.

Thank you all for being there for me.

If not me, then who?
If not now, then when?

Paraphrase of an ancient Jewish teaching

ABOUT THE AUTHOR

Dr. G. Eric Allenbaugh brings a wealth of personal and professional experience to the writing of this book. His warm, yet dynamic style gently engages others in examining their own life to both celebrate their successes and continue their journey to even greater life fulfillment. Since 1979, Eric has been president of his own consulting firm, which emphasizes individual peak performance and corporate excellence. His national and international clients include businesses, hospitals, all levels of government, and corporate boards.

He is a sought-after speaker on peak performance for both individuals and organizations. His personal and professional growth seminars are frequently described as "life-changing experiences" by the thousands of participants who have attended.

Prior to establishing his consulting practice, Eric was in hospital administration for a dozen years and became a Fellow of the American College of Healthcare Executives. His master's degree in hospital administration from UCLA was followed some years later by a University of Oregon doctorate that emphasized management, applied psychology, organization development, and health-care administration.

Eric and his wife reside in Lake Oswego, Oregon.

Part 1

WAKING
UP

Waking Up or Snoozing–
It's Your Call

"Every current experience
can aid you in your growth
toward higher consciousness—
if you know how to use it."

Ken Keyes

IN THE TWELFTH YEAR of my first marriage (does that tell you something?), my wife and I were vacationing in a quaint mountain cabin, complete with a warm fireplace and a beautiful river flowing by our view deck. With some hesitation in her voice, she said, "I've never liked our vacations!" All kinds of things went through my mind. Instead of pausing, listening, and seeking understanding, I became defensive. I said things like, "But you've helped plan our vacations! We've gone here and we've gone there. I can't believe you waited all these years to tell me this!"

To most people, that would have been a significant life wake-up call. Rather than addressing the real issue—our relationship—I chose to defend our vacations and reminded her that she actively participated in planning each of them! Instead of converting this teachable moment into a positive learning experience, I turned on my internal "snooze alarm." Neither willing nor able at that time in my life to receive and deal with that wake-up call, I continued sleepwalking through our relationship.

Three years later, she "surprised" me with an announcement of her desire to get a divorce. The message finally got through! While our marriage did not survive, I received an important and valuable gift. That wake-up call catapulted me on a new journey toward higher consciousness. And that costly gift, while initially difficult to receive, ultimately assisted me personally, professionally, and spiritually in experiencing life at a more fulfilling level.

"All of the significant battles are waged within the self."

Sheldon Kopp

Our life experience includes numerous *wake-up calls* and corresponding *choice points*. A wake-up call that is acted upon assists us in discovering a new level of awareness. With fresh insight, life's breakthrough moments can be converted into positive learning and growing experiences.

Each of us has "stuff" to work through. Facing our stuff can sometimes be too great, and we attempt to postpone reality. Rather than responding to the breakthrough moment and taking appropriate action, we may sleep through life's wake-up calls. We fight the learning by hitting our internal snooze alarm! As the world attempts to deliver a message, we resist by staying asleep and in our comfort zone. And the same messages keep repeating themselves until we get the learning.

Activating our snooze alarm temporarily assists us as a coping mechanism. Chronic *sleepwalking*, on the other hand, leads to major problems in our career, relationships, and life in general as teachable moments are locked out. Some of us merely go through the motions of life with our body in an upright position and our minds asleep to what is going on around us. Joining the ranks of the walking dead is a costly and unfulfilling way to experience life. By ignoring the series of little wake-up calls in my first marriage and practicing chronic relationship sleepwalking, I set myself up for a significant learning opportunity. Her departure, the inevitable large-scale wake-up call, certainly startled me into a process of becoming more aware—and of making better life choices.

Every situation presents us with an opportunity to automatically react or consciously respond: a *choice point*. The more aware we are, the more choices we have; the less aware, the fewer choices. By hearing, seeing, and feeling the many wake-up calls calling for attention, our work and home lives will be far more complete.

Life school provides us with many situations and corresponding choice points. We are a product of our choices, not of our circumstances. Given that, this book focuses on life strategies that enhance our awareness and assist us in making more accountable choices. By taking charge of our life at a higher level, we will experience more personal and professional fulfillment.

"Stay awake during the day and you'll sleep well at night."

Gay Hendricks

Many of us are not as awake as we can be. Yet the process of awakening, of learning, of discovering, is partially what life's about. How then do we increase our awareness? At the risk of oversimplifying, there are two strategies of awakening: the *traumatic commitment* and the *conscious commitment.*

A *significant emotional event* or wake-up call persuades us to view things differently. Wake-up calls come in many different forms, yet have one thing in common: They momentarily force us to interrupt the thought and behavioral patterns we normally practice. And those awareness shifts can lead to transformation. A divorce, getting fired, a major illness, losing a key client, flunking an important examination—these are the more traumatic methods of calling attention to important issues. Yet each contains a gift, if we are open to the learning.

A temptation exists to label wake-up calls as either positive or negative. Such categorization in itself can limit learning opportunities. Life events are actually neutral in expression; we give them meaning. An old story told to me by James Newton reinforces this concept:

Centuries ago, a farmer began his early morning chores only to discover that his prize horse had run away through a broken fence. A neighbor later said to him, "It's too bad that your prize horse ran away." The farmer replied, "Too bad? How do I know that the loss of the horse is a bad experience?"

Several days later, the prize horse returned—but not alone. With him were nearly a dozen of the finest wild horses that roamed the plains. Seeing the return of the prize horse together with the other horses, the neighbor came over and said to the farmer, "What good fortune you have experienced!" The farmer again replied, "Good fortune? How do I know that having all these horses is good fortune?"

The farmer's young adult son, obviously pleased with the new horses, selected one for his own. On his first attempt to ride bareback, however, the horse bucked violently, throwing the young man off and breaking his leg. Learning of the situation, the neighbor came over and said to the farmer, "What a terrible experience to have happened to your son." The farmer replied, "Terrible experience? How do I know that the breaking of my son's leg is a terrible experience?"

A week later, a vicious warlord came storming through the countryside, conscripting every able-bodied young man to fight in his bloody battles. The farmer's son was passed over. And so it goes.

How many times has something "bad" happened in your life that later turned out to be a springboard to greater learning? By looking beyond the immediate circumstances and being open to even more significant discovery, we can be our own internal resource for transformational learning.

Look for the learning.

Life's "gifts" of learning, growing, and self-correcting are often delivered in the form of a wake-up call. A timely wake-up call can be the catalyst for choosing a direction that serves you and those around you more effectively. Look for the learning in each of the following wake-up calls. Each teachable moment can be of service in your personal and professional growth—if you are open to receiving the "gift."

Look for the learning in each of the following *personal* wake-up calls:

- Getting a divorce
- Learning that your key relationship is viewed differently by your partner
- Having a child
- Experiencing a serious injury or illness
- Losing a friendship
- Having a "near-death" experience
- Having a "near-life" experience
- Discovering that a different culture does things better
- Experiencing kindness from someone you considered to be an enemy
- Discovering that God really exists
- Having unfinished business with someone who suddenly dies

- Receiving a registered letter from an unknown attorney
- Having another child
- Receiving a middle-of-the-night phone call about a family member
- Being invited to a socially important function
- Not being invited to a socially important function
- Becoming close friends with someone of another race
- Learning that a previously held position was wrong
- Discovering that your spouse is having an affair
- Meeting your spouse's lover and liking that person
- Receiving an important learning from a street derelict
- Going to your high school's twentieth reunion
- Meeting your new in-laws
- Learning that you cannot control everything
- Discovering that you can control much more than you thought
- Inheriting or receiving a large amount of money
- Filing for bankruptcy
- Looking in the mirror

Career and educational environments also provide numerous opportunities for discovering more about ourselves. Examine the following examples of *professional* wake-up calls. Perhaps one or more of these could serve as important breakthrough moments:

- Being passed over for promotion
- Receiving feedback saying that you have untapped potential
- Flunking an important examination

- Receiving a significant promotion
- Changing college majors or career paths
- Taking a sabbatical
- Studying a subject far outside of your field
- Generating an important, creative idea
- Being recognized as a master in your field
- Finding that your career ladder is "leaning up against the wrong wall"
- Acquiring a new boss who has very different expectations
- Getting fired or demoted
- Experiencing a major success
- Learning that your competitor has developed a major new product
- Moving to a new job or city
- Receiving a different performance evaluation than you expected
- Completing a major, important goal
- Accomplishing something you thought was beyond your capability
- Discovering that retirement is different than you anticipated

Systematic or conscious growth—commitment to lifelong learning—is yet another way of making a positive difference in our inner and outer world. Those who invest significantly in themselves generally experience much higher levels of life and career fulfillment than those who merely wait for learning opportunities to occur. As a conscious process, growth is accelerated when we are awake, aware, open, and willing to risk when confronted with a choice point.

"Success is not a destination that you ever reach. Success is the quality of your journey."

Jennifer James

Life is a learning and experiential process challenging you to apply your talents and sending wake-up calls when you don't. When your earthly life comes to a close, three important questions will likely be asked:

1. How much did you love?

2. What did you learn?

3. As a result of your being here, how is the world a better place?

How would you answer these questions? What would you learn if you were to take these questions seriously? What is your life's purpose? What do you want to accomplish in life? What do you want to master? How do you want to relate to others? How will you know when you are successful? How do you want to be remembered? The answers are within, and this book will assist you in tapping into those inner resources to experience an even more fulfilling life.

For more than a dozen years, I have been studying peak-performing individuals who achieve significant results while enjoying a sense of inner peace and fulfillment. Are these individuals any different from you and me? Not really. But they have learned to apply a number of practical, simple strategies that work in their own lives. And they have an unusual ability to tap into inner resources while functioning as a resource and role model to others.

The strategies employed by these peak performers are relatively simple and clearly transferable. We can learn from these people as they have learned from others. This book focuses on strategies you can use to create giants of yourself and others and to learn from those who convert these strategies into result-oriented behaviors. In observing life contributors, you are likely to witness these patterns:

- Clarity of and commitment to a personal mission and goals

- Lifelong growth and development, both personally and professionally

- A linking of head and heart—achieving balance—in the process of living life

- Creation and management of change

- The ability to learn from mistakes, self-correct, and move on

- A desire to give more than they take from life

- An approach that links their behavior to some meaningful purpose and core values

- Development of a strong sense of personal awareness and accountability

- Commitment to mastery of a talent or skill

- Development of both healthy independence and interdependence in relationships with others

- Empowerment of themselves and others—giant building

- The ability to communicate for understanding

- A commitment to function with integrity

- The ability to take care of themselves, physically and emotionally

- Development of a spiritual connection with the Source

- Risk, experimentation, and growth

- The expectation of positive results

- The ability to experience life to the fullest degree

"Transformation is the ability and willingness to live beyond your form."

Wayne Dyer

We are all learners or beginners in many respects. The focus of this book is conversion of teachable moments into positive learning and growing experiences. The messages between these covers are for leaders, followers, men, and women; there is something for each of us to learn and apply at work and at home.

Your journey into "inner space" through these chapters is intended to be fun, insightful, and practical. The transformation of your world starts from within and accelerates through a series of wake-up calls. This book explores practical strategies—choices—to enhance the quality of your own life while making an even greater contribution to your world. In the spirit of making a positive difference, read on and enjoy. Perhaps this book will serve as one of your "wake-up calls."

Stuck in Your Stuff:

WHAT IS THE LEARNING?

"When you are in a hole, stop digging."

Ian McIver

Stuff. We all have it! Relationship stuff. Self-esteem stuff. Sexual stuff. Career stuff. Financial stuff. And we get stuck from time to time. Getting stuck in our stuff usually signals that we have something to learn, and we don't want to face the learning! In the stuck-state cycle, which Wayne Dyer describes as "immobilization," behaviors might include total inaction, mild indecision, or simply the repetition of strategies that don't work. In this state, we limit our potential and generate inner stress. Explore these examples of stuck-state cycles as indicators of where immobilization might exist in your own life:

- You remain in an unsatisfying, unrewarding job.

- You don't make love as frequently and as passionately as you want.

- You repeatedly think about a negative experience with someone without actually confronting the issue directly.

- You withhold sharing what you are thinking, feeling, or wanting from your partner.

- You don't deal with unresolved conflict with an important person in your life.

- You remain bored or scared with the current situation rather than risking a new venture.

- You wake up frequently at night, churning about something that is bothering you.

- You stop yourself from reaching out to someone who appeals to you.

- You avoid giving important feedback to a special person.

- You continue to practice unhealthy health patterns.

- You avoid an important decision that needs to be made.

Every situation is brand-new.

An insightful definition of mental illness is "doing the same thing over and over—and expecting different results." I have been caught in that cycle myself from time to time, even while writing this book. Ironically, I experienced greater difficulty in writing this chapter than any other. And this chapter was the first I began to write. After many futile attempts to develop the concept, I finally put it aside and went on to other parts of the book. When I returned to this chapter, however, I pulled out my *same* notes to review what I had thought about previously—and again achieved the stuck state! Good grief! Another perfect lesson of doing the same thing over and over and expecting different results. The chapter finally got rolling when I put my old notes aside and moved into an entirely new thought process. Where would you benefit by putting aside old stuff?

We have the power to choose our response to any situation. Yet that choice is heavily influenced by how we view the world. Two types of choice-point filters have a profound impact on our response: those within and those outside of our control. Some choice influencers, such as sex and age, are outside of our control. Others, such as values and education, are within our control. Through conscious intention, we can empower and augment the elements that are within our control while minimizing the impact of those outside our control. How we view the world through our filters and how we respond at the choice point shapes both our present experience and our future options.

Choice-Point Filters

Outside My Control:

Race
Sex
Age
Country of origin
Birth family
Physical attributes
Raw intelligence
"Their" choices

Within My Control:

Feelings
Thoughts
Attitudes
Awareness
Values
Desire
Education
Knowledge
Training
Wellness
Risk taking
Principles
Creativity
Problem-solving skills

31

THE STUCK-STATE CYCLE
Behaviors and History Repeated!

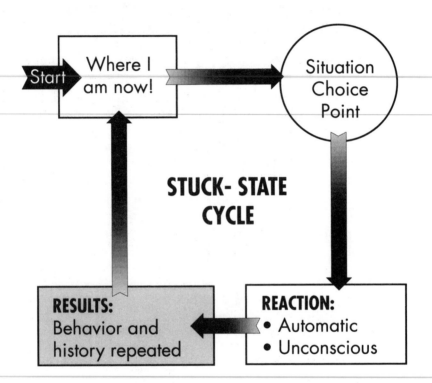

Let's explore the "stuck-state cycle." "Where I am now," the starting point, is a function of many factors, some of which we control and some of which are beyond our control. In traveling through life, "where I am now" reflects our choices. As in the saying "You cannot step in the same river twice," we constantly experience a new set of life conditions. New choice points, which we either control or delegate to external forces, continually become available.

Sometimes, however, we save up garbage from the past and allow it to influence and shape our present experience. Our gunnysack of old garbage gets bigger and heavier, yet we continue to add new stuff. Hanging on to the neck of the gunnysack, we throw it over our shoulder, drag old garbage into the present, and make out of the present—the past. By not letting go of the past, we re-create it and become stuck in our stuff. We recycle our old garbage.

"Everywhere I go, there I am again."

Pogo

History can be a great resource from which to learn and provide guidance in making current decisions. In a stuck state, however, our automatic, unconscious behaviors position us to react rather than respond to current choice points. As a result, history and old behaviors repeat. In dealing with a new situation by merely recycling old patterns, we re-create the past in the present. "Where I am now" merely recycles where I was before, and things start becoming very familiar! When we recycle our internal garbage, the heap gets larger and spills over into other areas of our life.

Consider the dinosaur. This prehistoric animal "mastered" maintaining the status quo in a changing environment. Rather than adapting to or even influencing its environment, the dinosaur simply remained on automatic pilot until it became extinct. Doing the same thing over and over became a dysfunctional stuck-state cycle. And we know what happened to the dinosaur.

Think about an irritating behavior that your partner, co-worker, or child does with some regularity—one of your "hot buttons." When you experience this behavior, chances are that you react—and perhaps in the same way each time. Maybe one of your children, after taking a shower, leaves damp towels on the carpeted floor. When you discover the towel, you go into a tirade! "How many times do I have to tell you to hang your towel up or put it in the hamper? Next time, put your towel away!" You have experienced this situation at least twenty times and

33

reacted with similar automatic, unconscious behaviors. Interestingly enough, a part of you knows that this reaction does not work, yet you unconsciously choose a stuck-state pattern that puts even more transgressions into your gunnysack. And you end up where you were before. You are now positioned to restart the same stuck-state cycle.

AFTER I DREW THE STUCK-STATE ILLUSTRATION on chart paper in one of my seminars, an executive approached me during a break. Pointing to the chart, he asked, "Can I have that?" I wrote a short note on the chart and handed it to him. To my surprise, tears streamed down his cheeks. I asked him to share his thoughts with me. He said, "I have been fired from my last *nine* jobs." (What he didn't know was that he was about to be fired from his tenth job. His boss had shared that with me just prior to the seminar.) He went on to explain, "Every time, my boss was a jerk. My boss didn't understand me. My boss didn't give me clear direction. My boss didn't give me feedback. My boss didn't respect me. My boss . . ." He went on to describe several other reasons why his various bosses were unsatisfactory or just incompetent. "And you know what?" he continued, "I am working for another jerk!" According to my calculations, that equals ten jerks in a row. Statistically, the probability of working for that many consecutive jerks remains remarkably slim.

He then became very quiet and more tears flowed. "It wasn't my bosses at all—it was me. I created those results," he concluded. "For the first time, I can now see how I set myself up to get fired. Your diagram is right on target." What a wake-up call!

Now that he was confronted with an important career choice point, he accepted the challenge of doing things differently in his life. As a reminder to continue his growth journey, the stuck-state diagram now hangs on his office wall. Rather than continuing to function on automatic pilot, he taught himself to pause, self-correct, and stretch into new behaviors. His new patterns of behavior demonstrated such growth that his boss chose to give him a new opportunity. He continued to work with that boss for several more years and became a source of encouragement to others. Wake-up calls. Choice points.

When we are in the reactive or automatic mode, problems are placed "out there." We become victims of others' actions. Instead of using creative resources to work through a situation, we divert our creativity toward blaming external circumstances and conditions. As long as we continue to blame others, we remain ignorant about our contribution to the problem or what we can do differently to bring about a better result. We give up our power, our control, and our ability to influence or shape life experiences. We neglect the issues that need attention and stop growing. All meaningful change comes from within. By placing the problem "out there," we delegate power to external forces, which ultimately shape our destiny.

When you sleepwalk through relationships, be prepared for unexpected wake-up calls.

AFTER MY FIRST MARRIAGE "went away," I blamed my former wife for the demise of our relationship. From my warped perspective at the time, the problem clearly was centered "out there." After fifteen years of marriage, how could she just decide to leave without talking through the issues? For 2 ½ years after our divorce, I focused on her lack of communication, her unfairness, and her lack of loyalty. In this unconscious mode, I avoided working on my own stuff! I found it easier to blame her than to deal with the parts of my own life that were calling for attention. (It is easier by far to find the flaws in others than to deal with our own.) Outside of my awareness, I moved into a stuck state.

What we focus on determines what we miss. I focused on the shortcomings of my wife and on how unfairly I had been treated. I was stuck on *her* stuff—stuff over which I had little or no control. In this self-righteous state, I missed working through my own stuff—stuff over which I had a great deal of control! **35**

Her departure became one of my life's more important wake-up calls. Because I was not ready to receive the message, however, I activated my internal snooze alarm. At this important choice point, I convinced myself to continue sleepwalking for another several years rather than doing the inner work that needed attention. Somehow, keeping the issues "out there" appeared safer than facing my inner work.

In the stuck-state cycle, we deny our opportunity to grow by automatically reacting at the choice point. We repeat behaviors that historically have not worked, yet we expect a different outcome. Lacking the courage to look within, we empower external forces to take charge of our lives. By attempting to change our outside world, we ignore the inner work requiring attention. As a result, we end up where we started—and the cycle repeats.

When you reach your next important choice point, listen to your self-talk. If you are debating whether or not to take charge of your life, ask yourself these important questions:

AWARENESS CHECKS

- What is the *worst* that could happen if I worked on my own stuff?

- What is the *best* that could happen if I worked on my own stuff?

- What if I *don't* work on my own stuff?

- What do I gain or lose by continuing to sleepwalk?

- What is the learning for me?

Every choice moves you toward something, draws you away from something, or locks you into a stuck-state pattern. In most cases, you hold yourself back. Self-imposed limits have nothing to do with heredity and environment. Continuing to cling to the patterns you know inhibits your ability to discover what you don't know. When you empower self-limiting beliefs, you limit your potential. When you argue for your limitations, all you get is your limits—and you stay stuck. Behavior, then, becomes a function of choices, not conditions or circumstances.

Wake-up calls and choice points can make an important and positive difference in your life. Acknowledge them as gifts waiting to be opened. The more aware you are, the more options that are available. Awareness attracts alternatives and resources. The decision to address your stuck-state issues is a decision to be set free. You are the chooser, and now is the time.

Getting Unstuck:
YOUR CHOICE POINTS

"Our history is not our destiny."

Alan Cohen

Every moment and every situation provides a new choice—an opportunity to do things differently and produce even better results. Yet we human beings are funny critters. If something *doesn't* work in our life, we tend to repeat that behavior! Nathaniel Branden, in his book *Honoring the Self* (1983), said it succinctly: "We are the one species that is able to form a judgment about what is best for us to do—and then proceed to do the opposite." Even though the answers are within us regarding most life situations, we tend to ignore what we know; we depress our intuition and even disregard our own values, sleepwalking through our choice points. The result? More of the same—history is repeated.

A W A R E N E S S   C H E C K S

- Where are you repeating history in your life?

- Are you producing the same results when you know that more desirable outcomes could be achieved?

- Do you know more about effective communication than you actually practice?

- Are you better at building quality relationships than you actually practice?

- Do you know more about resolving conflicts equitably than your behaviors suggest?

- What is the learning here?

The chances are good that a gap exists between what you *know* and what you *do*. Rather than worrying about that gap, however, explore the learning.

We are a product of our choices, not of our circumstances.

I AM REMINDED OF AN OLD STORY about twin brothers reared in an abusive, alcoholic family environment. Both parents were marginally functional, frequently out of work, and physically abusive to the twin boys. After neighbors called in the Children's Services Division, the courts removed the boys from this chaotic home environment. Both boys went their independent ways, separately assigned to various foster homes.

More than three decades passed before they had contact with one another. And their circumstantial reunion was eventful. As one brother left his twenty-second-story law office one evening, he was approached by a shabbily dressed, alcoholic street person begging for a handout. While the attorney reached into his pocket for loose change, their eyes met and a vague sense of familiarity came over both of them. The ensuing conversation resulted in each discovering his long-lost twin brother.

Now worlds apart, they once shared the same womb and the same family environment. The alcoholic brother defensively argued for his position in life. "How could you expect me to be any different? Look, Mom and Dad were alcoholics. They treated me like dirt, and it was clear that I was unwanted. I learned early to drink and had to steal just to survive. Life has been tough, but I am a survivor. I had no choice but to hit the streets."

The lawyer brother had an entirely different perspective. "Although our folks were alcoholics and were abusive to us as well as to each other, I decided early on that I was going to do things differently. I didn't want alcohol to ruin my life as it did theirs, so I stayed away from drinking. I also learned that I needed to approach relationships differently, so I have invested in my own development through therapy, school, seminars, and books. While I still have some work to do, my life seems to be going quite well."

Twin brothers, coming from the same heredity and environment, obviously made different choices. One automatically settled for "survival" and was a "victim" of tough life circumstances. The other, coming from the same situation, chose "life" and took responsibility for his decisions. You are probably familiar with many similar stories about people in tough circumstances who respond to the challenge rather than succumbing to external forces. Someone once said, "It's not the hand you are dealt, it's how you play the cards that makes the difference."

Every situation provides us with a new choice point. By identifying when we are at a choice point and tending to our inner work, we position ourselves to influence our circumstances instead of becoming victims of them. When we consciously choose how we respond, we positively influence the **41** nature of the results and grow in the process. We shape our future rather than being shaped by it.

When we reach a new choice point, we can either *react* and drop into the stuck state or *respond* and experience the learning. The difference between reacting and responding can be likened to our response to a prescription drug. We don't want to react to the medication; that worsens the situation. Instead, we want our body to respond favorably to the medication and receive its full value. The same is true in life: We must consciously explore the full value of our choices.

"Circumstances do not determine a man, they reveal him."

James Allen

We are a product of our choices, not of our circumstances. The whole course of our human experience is linked to our decisions. Not all of our choices, however, are made out of full awareness. When we slip into automatic pilot, things "just seem to happen to us." This "unconscious" part of us, according to Will Schutz (1979), is simply "all those things of which we choose not to be aware." As long as we perceive the cause to be "out there," our creative energies are diverted to blaming, criticizing, rationalizing, justifying, explaining, avoiding, and attempting to change external forces. These forces are empowered, and our options become fewer through this self-limiting process. Avoiding learning opportunities often requires more energy than actually confronting our stuck-state issues. Choosing to stay stuck in our stuff delegates the shaping of our destiny to external forces.

If we have survived with our past patterns and practices, we sometimes resist doing things differently. Quality living, however, cannot be experienced at the survival level. Settling for survival makes it impossible to experience life at a more fulfilling level. Most of us want more joy, peace of mind, enlightenment,

EVERY SITUATION IS BRAND-NEW!
CHOICE: Grow or repeat history

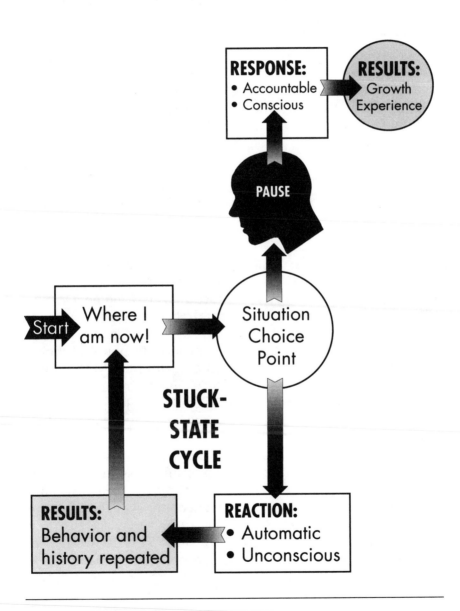

personal and professional satisfaction, prosperity, spiritual connection, and wellness. None of these higher levels can be attained by settling for survival.

When we accept the responsibility for choosing our response to life situations, we empower internal rather than external forces. Everything becomes different when we choose to take control rather than be controlled. We experience a new sense of freedom, growth, and energy. We begin moving off our position and into new territory: our stretch zone. We learn, grow, and create new options and begin to make a positive difference in our life.

Don't just do something, sit there.

Moving out of our stuck state requires us to risk and be willing to do things differently. The most critical first step at a choice point is to *pause!* More than just a moment in time, the choice-point moment requires us to become quiet inside and allow our internal resources to assist us in making a positive difference. All advances in life come through the power of choice.

Most of the time, the answers are within us, yet we often ignore the value of these internal resources by automatically acting. You have heard the expression: "Don't just sit there, *do* something!" Pausing takes the opposite path: "Don't just do something, *sit* there." Pausing enables us to tap into our intuitive, rational, and spiritual resources. In neurolinguistic programming terms, the pause becomes an important "break state." By consciously moving from the stuck state to the break state, we find that growth opportunities become available. Pausing accelerates our awakening.

When we liberate ourselves from past patterns, we are free to explore new options. Accepting responsibility enables us to gain control. This accountable, conscious process is activated first with a pause, followed by exploring these questions:

AWARENESS CHECKS

- What am I not facing in my life—what am I resisting?

- What is the learning for me?

- What do I really want?

- What can I do or say right now that will make a positive difference?

Letting go of past habits and patterns requires awareness, commitment, and risk taking. In the stuck-state mode, it is easier to blame external elements than to accept responsibility. Moving into our personal growth zone requires self-examination rather than "other" examination. To assist in experiencing this positive growth, follow these break-state strategies:

- Teach yourself to pause at the choice point and tap into your inner resources. The answers are within.

- Determine what you want to create in your life, and set specific written behavioral goals.

- Clarify your values and principles that can serve as guides in decision making at the choice point.

- Share your goals with a trusted friend and ask for assistance and periodic feedback related to behavioral progress.

- Maintain a confidential journal on your stuck-state and break-state choices. Your mind processes written information differently from just thinking about available choices. Your journal can be an important resource in tracking your progress.

45

- Replace "This is the way I am" with "Up until now . . ." or "I am now choosing . . ." This reflective process reinforces pausing at the choice point and encourages self-awareness.

- Once a week, review your choices in order to celebrate successes and take appropriate corrective action. Be gentle with yourself; this process is about self-correction, not perfection.

"Life does not happen to us, it happens from us."

Mike Wickett

ONE OF MY MOST POWERFUL LEARNINGS about choice points occurred when I was just fifteen years old. In 1959, I was a sophomore at a large high school in Southern California. The student body of 3,200 was a melting pot of racial groups, with about one-third African-American, one third Hispanic, and the remaining third a mixture of white and Asian. The environment was tough. Commonplace on campus were various weapons such as knives, pipes, chains, brass knuckles, and an occasional zip gun. Fights and gang activity were weekly events.

After a football game in the fall of 1959, I left the bleachers with my girlfriend. As we walked down the crowded sidewalk, someone kicked me from behind. When I turned around, I discovered a gang called Los Lobos, armed with brass knuckles. The first blow of the unprovoked attack broke my nose, one of several bones to be broken in the pounding. Fists came from every direction as they surrounded me. In addition to the fractures, I experienced a brain concussion and internal bleeding. Surgery was eventually required to repair one of the injuries I sustained. The treating physician advised me that if I had been hit in the head one more time, I probably would have died.

Because so many people were being attacked by gangs, school administrators eventually ended Friday night football games. In this stressful environment, many students exhibited stuck-state behaviors related to issues of interracial conflict. Tensions ran high as people continuously repeated patterns that clearly did not work.

After I recovered medically, some friends approached me and said, "Let's go get those guys!" That was the way problems were "resolved." When people were attacked, evening the score became a priority, and the cycle of problems continued. I was being provided with the opportunity of securing revenge, and a part of me said, "Yes!" The sweet taste of revenge was clearly an option at that point.

Another part of me paused and said, "No!" Revenge does not work. Clearly, history had demonstrated time and time again at that high school that revenge only accelerated and intensified the conflict. Escalation of hostilities would only reinforce a stuck-state cycle and generate the same negative results. We needed to do something differently. We needed someone to break the counterproductive chain of events.

Confronted with the choice point of getting even or initiating a new strategy, I chose to pursue the "road less travelled." With members of various ethnic groups, I put together what we called a "Brotherhood Committee" to work on enhancing racial relationships. I was amazed to learn how much interest fellow students had in building a brighter future, especially since this occurred before the major racial equality movement in the United States. More and more students joined in the effort to make a positive difference.

Two years later, I ran for student body president—still pursuing the enhancement of student relationships. Even though I ran against two friends, one a football hero and the other a popular "big man on campus," a significant majority of the 3,200 students joined me in the process of doing things differently. I will not claim that the racial problems were resolved—they were not. We did, however, make significant progress in building bridges between cultures, learning how to talk with and relate to different ethnic groups, resolving differences without resorting

47

to violence, and learning to build trust in the most difficult of circumstances.

Every moment and every situation is brand-new. Although it was one of my more difficult life experiences, the gang attack became one of my more powerful learning opportunities. Choosing to pause and respond rather than reacting altered my own experience and eventually influenced the environment in which I lived. I discovered at an early age that we are a product of our choices, not of our circumstances, and that by making conscious, aware choices, we can positively influence our circumstances.

Every choice moves us closer to or farther away from something. Where are your choices taking your life? What do your behaviors demonstrate that you are saying yes to or no to in life? While you do not necessarily choose your situation, you choose your current experience and future. You are free until the moment a choice is made; then you become the product of that choice point. Since all advances in life come through the power of choice, pause first and explore the options before acting. Address your inner work at the choice-point moment and you will position yourself to influence rather than be a victim of circumstances.

Simply put, a choice point provides us with an opportunity to react or respond. When we react, our "repeat button" remains stuck in the "on" position. Behaviors are automatically recycled, even though the results may not serve us well. When we respond, the conscious pause enables us to activate our "reset button," self-correct, and experience the learning. Recognizing our choice points and self-correcting becomes a transformational process in which we move from sleepwalking to an awakened state. Making the most of life's breakthrough moments enables us to grow while experiencing greater joy and fulfillment. Convert your wake-up calls into gifts.

Resistance:
A RESOURCE IN DISGUISE

"We meet ourselves time and again in a thousand disguises on the path of life."

Carl Jung

As long as we continue to place blame "out there," we stay stuck in our stuff. The moment we determine the cause to be outside of ourselves, we limit our growth. And history repeats itself, bringing our stuff into sharp focus once again. The same lessons keep repeating until we get the learning.

Dealing with what you resist takes courage and self-awareness. Yet the process of self-examination helps you to determine where you are now, where you want to be, and how to get there.

The choice you make to deal with what you resist is a choice to make a positive difference both within yourself and in your interaction with others.

What do you resist in life? In your relationships? In your work situation? What ideas do you automatically oppose? When someone you don't particularly respect brings up an idea, how do you respond? How good are you at finding the flaws in the ideas of others? Resistance comes with the territory of life.

Your greatest opportunity to learn and grow can come from the areas you resist. Resistance can be good feedback and may be a disguised gift. Learn to look for the gift. Pay attention to the areas you resist—wake-up calls abound! People often resist intimacy, trusting, risking, being vulnerable, being "present," moving off their position, sharing feelings, and being spontaneous. Individuals create conditions that enable them to stay within their comfort zone, and comfort zones limit growth. Breaking through resistance enables you to grow.

As a seminar exercise, I often request participants to select a partner and identify who will be person "A" and person "B" for the purpose of demonstrating a principle. They face each other with hands palm to palm, and person "A" is instructed to safely push on person "B's" palms. What does person "B" do? He or she resists automatically, even though no instruction to oppose was given.

The typical human response is to resist pressure. Upon experiencing resistance, person "A" simply pushes harder. This is also a typical response. Eventually the one who pushes the hardest "wins," or so it seems.

Pay attention to resistance. When others resist a direction in which you want to go or an idea you want to pursue, it is a common strategy to push harder until "they" go along. Their consent on the outside, however, typically camouflages resistance on the inside. And *they* (not you, of course) keep score! They remember! Getting even or *leveling* generally results. Three months later, you may have another idea, and it's stonewalled! You "won" last time; now it's their turn to win.

Resistance from external sources can provide important information to assist you in identifying what requires attention.

By paying attention to resistance, you can gain insights, develop alternative approaches, increase empathy for others, and learn new ways to develop rapport. View resistance as a resource and new perspectives and positive alternatives will emerge.

Picture someone with whom you are currently experiencing conflict or difficulties. From your perspective, what is that person resisting? What could he or she do differently to enhance effectiveness or to enable your relationship to work even better? What *other* people need to do differently is so obvious. That same clarity does not always apply to ourselves.

"That which you resist persists."

Now, what do *you* resist? The typical human responses are to *attack* or *avoid*. Neither works well, yet these are the strategies that are most frequently employed. Ignoring wake-up calls keeps us ignorant of our opportunities to improve. Human beings are strange! Every other creature in the animal kingdom with any intuitive ability listens to the signals and does whatever it needs to do to take care of itself. And we do the opposite!

Martial arts employ resistance as a strategic positive force. In judo, for example, resistance exerted by an opponent coupled with harmonious actions on your part gives you a distinct advantage. Swimming *with* rather than *against* the current is yet another example of using resistance as a positive force. Resistance has been acknowledged as a resource for thousands of years. Yet we still struggle with the concept.

"That which you resist persists." This message has challenged people for thousands of years. It suggests that the same problem is sent to you over and over again until you experience the gift of learning. Once you "get it," the lesson need not be sent again.

A MINISTER PREACHED THE SAME SERMON five Sundays in a row. After the third repetitive sermon, people talked busily in the parking lot about this strange phenomenon. After the fourth Sunday, the elders met to discuss the situation. After the fifth, a special board meeting challenged the minister about his recurring sermon. He replied, "I'm glad you noticed! I'm going to keep on preaching the same sermon every Sunday until you get it!" Sometimes we simply ignore important wake-up calls, yet we wonder why the same things "keep happening to us."

Even as you read this book, you will probably experience resistance to some of the ideas and life strategies it contains. The harder you fight or avoid, the less likely it is that you will experience the gift. I don't expect or even want you to agree with everything in these chapters, yet I encourage your open exploration. A reason exists for you to read this book, and I invite you to discover this gift.

Rather than attacking the messages or avoiding the wake-up calls, I ask you to *pause.* Acknowledge the wall of resistance, and be willing to explore the learning. Imagine resistance as a wall separating you from important learning on the other side. Instead of attacking or avoiding the wall, cut a doorway and step through that wall of resistance. By exploring what is on the other side, you will experience your greatest growth.

Resistance is a resource in disguise. Look for the gift. Step through the wall of resistance and discover the learning.

The Dirty Dozen:
ESCAPING ACCOUNTABILITY

*"Increased self awareness begins
with a commitment to
look inside."*

Will Schutz

Accountability involves claiming your own power and using internal resources to create even better results in life. Accountability consciously influences the effects of new situations by claiming the power to ask, "What can I do right now that would make a positive difference?" Accountable behavior enables you to take charge of your thoughts, feelings, and actions, regardless of the actions of others, and to experience life at a more fulfilling level.

Escaping accountability—and each of us has weaseled out of taking responsibility from time to time—can occur consciously or unconsciously.

The "Dirty Dozen" listed below describe how other people escape accountability. Surely, *you* would not follow these practices!

1. I had no choice!

2. I had no control!

3. I don't know!

4. I forgot!

5. I'll try!

6. If . . . , then . . . !

7. Nobody told me!

8. It's not my fault!

9. It's not my job!

10. I can't!

11. That's just the way I am!

12. I'll wait and see!

1. "I had no choice!"

At a seminar I conducted for a large group of student leaders, a young man stated, "I had no choice but to take drugs. Everybody was taking drugs!" Denying the option of a choice avoids accountability. You *always* have a choice, even though you may not like its consequences. Paying taxes, for example, is a choice. The consequences of *not* paying your taxes, however, can be significant.

The day following the U.S. attack on Libya in 1986, President Reagan announced: "We had no choice but to bomb Libya." We had no choice? Of course we had a choice. He went on to say that we had exhausted all other alternatives before making the decision to attack. We were not, however, even on speaking terms with Libya; we had severed diplomatic relations long before we chose to use military force. The bombing occurred in retaliation for Libya's alleged involvement in a terrorist attack on a German disco, resulting in the deaths of American servicemen. We later learned that Libya was not involved with that particular terrorist issue. Libya's nonaccountability in other situations is not the issue; the issue focuses on our own nonaccountability.

We can influence the accountability of others without controlling it. We do have control, however, over our own accountability. And by choosing inner accountability, we can—in most cases—positively influence others.

2. "I had no control!"

"The devil made me do it" is a far-reaching excuse to escape accountability. If, in fact, the devil really made you do it, then a whole new set of problems must be explored!

I am reminded of a married couple in the middle of a major argument. Harsh words are flying back and forth. Both of them are "out of control" with anger. The telephone rings. It's the minister! Notice how the voice tone changes as the spouse calmly and pleasantly chats with the minister. When the telephone conversation ends, the receiver slams down and screaming resumes; they are again "out of control." Out of control? No! This behavior commands control and uses anger as a power tool. To claim "I had no control" excuses accountability.

3. "I don't know!"

Two kinds of "I don't know" are generally practiced: one factual, the other nonaccountable. For example, I don't know how to speak Russian. This was brought into sharp focus when I worked in the former Soviet Union and translators were required for communication.

The second kind of "I don't know" is nonaccountable. We sometimes claim not to know something when, in our heart of

55

hearts, we do. We cannot or will not deal with the real issue and so we use the "I don't know" technique as an excuse to let ourselves off the hook. For example, my first wife's announcement of her departure came as a "surprise." Fifteen years of marriage, and she just decided to leave. No warning, no discussions, no significant effort to improve our relationship. For a while, I convinced myself and others that her decision came completely out of the blue. Wrong!

In my heart of hearts, I had known for years that our relationship lacked depth. At that stage of development in my life, I was partially unwilling and partially unable to deal well with difficult relationship issues. Ignoring them became the easy way out. Nonaccountable!

Claiming that we know when we actually don't demonstrates yet another variation of nonaccountability. Sometimes we claim to know how someone else feels when we really don't. Or we might say we understand when we really think the other person is on another planet! To say that we don't know when we really do or to claim that we know when we really don't are both forms of digging ourselves into a deeper hole. Choose to stop digging the hole deeper.

Interacting with individuals who frequently state: "I don't know" can be a frustrating experience. I have often asked, "If you did know, what would the answer be?" Amazingly, 80 percent of the time these same individuals respond with one or more options that only moments before seemed inaccessible in their problem-solving process. Choosing not to know is nonaccountable.

4. "I forgot!"

A significant difference exists between genuinely forgetting and choosing not to remember! One of our teenage sons frequently "forgot" to do his chores, but without fail, he remembered allowance day and the precise amount of the allowance! I am amazed that he could remember those two points and forget to do his chores. To assist him in "remembering," we developed a new system for paying his allowance. Part of his allowance became automatic; the other part related to the quality and completion of his responsibilities. In addition, he was to evaluate his own effectiveness in doing the chores and to determine whether he qualified for the full amount. Building in accountability works.

To say that we forgot when we chose not to remember avoids accountability. A variation of this theme involves becoming so busy doing things that we want to do that we "forget" to tend to the matters that are considered important by others.

5. "I'll try!"

To demonstrate this point in a seminar, I asked a participant to "try" to pick up a pen held in my hand. She reached out and picked it up. I said, "No, you picked up the pen. I asked you to *try* to pick it up." Now that she understood my instruction, she strained and groaned as she "tried" unsuccessfully to pick up the pen. The point: Either we pick up the pen or we don't. When we have no intention of following through, trying becomes a futile effort.

If you invited a couple over for dinner, how would you feel if they responded by saying, "We'll try to be there." What are they going to do—drive around your block several times *trying* to get to your house? Either they come to dinner or they don't. The same goes for delegation of a task. When someone says, "I'll try to get this done," pause and clarify. What do they intend? Are they planning to do the assignment or put it off? A clear response is required—a definite yes or no. In fact, many people are much more open to hearing a definite "No" than a noncommittal "I'll try." A nonaccountable response, in addition to creating confusion and tension in a relationship, discounts the credibility of the speaker. The costs of nonaccountability are high.

6. "If . . . , then . . . !"

A young supervisor once said to me, "If they pay me more money, then I will work harder and do higher-quality work." What are the chances of that individual being paid more money? Zip! Why would an employer want to pay more to someone who holds back on productivity and quality? What if, instead, that

57

individual chose to work harder and perform with higher quality? Such long-term efforts would more likely be rewarded with increased compensation.

Another person shared with me: "If I were in a relationship, then I would be happy." Who wants to be in a relationship with an unhappy person? Why would someone seek out an unhappy person with the intent of making him or her happy? This strategy simply does not work well. A far more effective approach involves *being* happy—then the probability of developing a quality relationship greatly improves!

The "if-then" strategy places conditions between us and our goals, conditions that distance us from those goals. Perhaps the conditions become more important than the goals, or perhaps we don't really want our stated goals—we want something else that will keep us in our comfort zone. For example, we say, "If you do this, then I will trust you." We set up hoops for people to jump through. After they do this, then do we trust them? Maybe yes, maybe no. The more typical response is to create new hoops.

If you are serious about your goals, drop the conditions. Go directly to your goal. Be your goal! Conditions often disguise strategies for escaping accountability. Why not just take charge and create the experience you are looking for? As the Nike motto states: "Just do it."

7. "Nobody told me!"

Peter, our oldest son, came home from high school somewhat distressed and said, "Dad, we had a calculus midterm today, and nobody told me." I asked, "Pete, did anyone else in the class know about the examination?" "Oh yes, they all knew. But nobody told me!"

I have frequently heard people say, "I don't know what my boss thinks of my performance. In fact, I have not had a performance review in years." Good grief! Performance feedback is critical to your development, promotions, and career future. If you don't know what your boss thinks of your performance, find out! Do your own performance evaluation, then make an appointment with your boss to review your strengths and opportunities for improvement. You cannot afford not to know. To simply complain about the lack of feedback is nonaccountable. Leave your comfort zone and get the information you need. It's your career. Care enough to take action.

Having guided thousands of executives through this process of self-appraisal and feedback with the boss, I have found the results to be overwhelmingly positive. Most bosses genuinely appreciate an associate's initiative in claiming responsibility for self-assessment and simplifying the performance-feedback loop. In simple terms, if you don't know how your boss feels about your performance, take the responsibility of finding out!

Sleepwalking through life and relationships, not being fully present, and not listening with every bone in our body results in our losing touch with reality. And then, with great non-accountability, we announce: "Nobody told me." Periodically solicit relationship feedback from your spouse or partner and performance feedback from your boss. If you shovel while the piles are small, relationships and careers seem to work better—and you won't have any reason to say: "Nobody told me."

8. "It's not my fault!"

When we blame others, we prevent ourselves from learning. We block out important growth information and end up empowering outside forces, while we remain ignorant about how we contributed to the situation. Yes, there are times when something is legitimately not our fault. Blaming others, however, keeps us in a stuck state and is ultimately rough on our own self-esteem.

An extreme application of "It's not my fault" can be found in most prisons. Studies of inmates' attitudes concluded that only 3 percent accepted accountability for their choices. When they were asked why they were in prison, inmates each responded with their own "It's not my fault" story. One typical inmate said, **59**

"While we were robbing a bank [does that give you a clue?], I was in charge of cracking the vault. My partner was supposed to be on the lookout for cops. We each had walkie-talkies. When the cops came, he ran and left me there. It's not my fault I'm in prison; my partner let me down." Blaming others escapes accountability and enables us to avoid dealing with issues. Instead of focusing on nonaccountable fault finding, ask, "What's the learning for me?" Or, as Anthony Robbins says in his *Personal Power* audiotapes, "What's not perfect—yet?"

9. "It's not my job!"

SEVERAL YEARS AGO, I ATTENDED a seminar on peak performance taught by Ken Blanchard, coauthor of *The One Minute Manager*. My guest at the seminar was Darrel Hume, a vice president at Nordstrom. This context is important, as the seminar itself was held in a hotel that was in bankruptcy. The service was terrible. During the smorgasbord-style lunch, I noticed that the one-gallon salad dressing containers had no scoops. Since picking up a gallon container to pour a small amount of dressing on a salad was beyond my ability, I decided to ask one of the waiters to take care of the situation. A hotel waiter, leaning against the wall only six feet from the salad dressing, seemed like the appropriate person to resolve the problem. I advised him of the situation and requested his assistance. With his arms folded, he looked at me and said, "It's not my job!" He didn't do salad dressing spoons. I looked at him and said, "Perfect. No wonder your hotel is bankrupt!" He didn't have the slightest idea what I was talking about.

One would never hear "It's not my job" at Nordstrom, IBM, Les Schwab Tire Service, Honda of America, or Federal Express. When it comes to customer service and quality products, nothing seems to be outside of the job description of associates. In fact, you are more likely to hear "It *is* my job!" at these organizations. And look at the positive long-term results they achieve.

What is "outside" of your job description at work and at home? Are you placing limits on yourself and others by claiming "It's not my job"? What career development and relationship costs do you experience with these limits? What if you unplugged the stops at work and at home and did whatever it takes to make things hum?

10. "I can't!"

Henry Ford once said, "If you think you can, or if you think you can't, you're right!" We frequently determine our outcome in advance, then behave in ways that support our predetermined conclusions.

We might say "I can't" when we mean "I won't." This escapes accountability and leaves others wondering about our credibility. Before you say "I can't" to yourself or others, pause. Is it true that you can't, or is it that you won't? "I can't balance a checkbook; numbers and I just don't get along." "I can't make our relationship work." "I can't exercise three times a week." "I can't accept that major assignment from my boss." Be clear about your choice points—and take charge of your life. Bob Moawad, a national consultant, stated, "Success comes in cans!"

Another complaint I frequently hear from executives is: "I don't have the authority to do my job!" In a significant majority of these cases, they clearly have the authority, yet do not claim it. Claiming to be unable to do a job because of a lack of authority more often than not merely reflects a lack of courage to do what needs to be done. Rather than claiming personal power and taking prudent risks, a smoke screen is substituted. Grace Hopper, a gutsy admiral in the U.S. Navy, said, "It is easier to ask for forgiveness than to ask for permission." She clearly did not understand when younger officers protested: "I can't."

11. "That's just the way I am!"

"Announcement! Announcement! I am fully complete. I am fully educated. I do not need any more opportunities for growth and development. What you see is what you get!" This nonaccountable strategy justifies an unwillingness to move off our position and puts the responsibility on others to make a difference. Either we are green and growing or ripe and rotting. "That's just the

61

way I am" announces that we are dead on the vine. Our philosophy, attitudes, behaviors, and perspectives are fixed. People end up having to work around us rather than with us, and we become obstacles. Significant costs, for ourselves and others, result from this locked-in position.

12. "I'll wait and see!"

I have seen a few attendees at my leadership seminars choose to sit in the back row with their arms folded, saying through their behavior, "I'll wait and see if this is going to be a good seminar." (Incidentally, this is an example of followership, not leadership.) The responsibility is clearly up to someone else—me, in this case—to make it a good seminar. Sometimes these people choose the same "I'll wait and see" approach in other life areas. "I'll wait and see how this relationship goes." "I'll wait and see how my new boss works out." "I'll wait and see what life will be like!" As the self-appointed skeptical observers of life, they look for and find the flaws and hold back their support and involvement. When things do not work out well, and they seldom do, these people come away with the satisfaction of saying, "I told you so!"

You cannot escape your life issues. Why not transform them?

We create our own experience in life and can generally find what we are looking for. In this "Dirty Dozen" strategy, the responsibility is clearly up to others to prove that they can fulfill our unspoken expectations. When they do not, the "I'll wait and see" folks move in with surgical precision, expose the flaw, and again settle into their back seat.

Are you placing the responsibility on others to create the experience you are seeking? This approach sets you up for a series of disappointments. In the grand scheme of things, not many people will commit to fulfilling your needs over theirs. If you are waiting for *them* to make a positive difference in your life, be prepared for a lifetime wait. Seldom do you exceed your self-expectations.

While many creative ways exist to escape accountability, the Dirty Dozen lists the most common ones. Which are your favorites? Be honest, you must have used one or more of them once in a while. Maybe you can add some "accountability escapers" to the list, such as "I don't have time." Of course you have time. In fact, each of us has exactly the same amount of time—twenty-four hours in a day. *How* we choose to spend our time becomes the issue. Another might be: "I didn't mean to . . ." If we choose to be more sensitive to others, the feeble excuse "I didn't mean to . . ." will not have to be offered.

Conscious or unconscious efforts to escape accountability eventually result in a personal or professional wake-up call. When you choose to take charge of your thoughts, feelings, and actions, wake-up calls are less likely to occur.

AWARENESS CHECKS

- Where might you be escaping accountability?
- If you don't take charge, who will?
- If this isn't the best time, when will you decide to take action?
- What is the learning right now?

CHAPTER

6

New Address–
Same Old Stuff!

**"Live out of your imagination,
not your history."**

Stephen R. Covey

A FEW YEARS BACK, I had a sports car that few mechanics were skilled enough to service. Through other sports car enthusiasts, I learned about a talented mechanic who operated out of a small service station. I asked him to work on my car and I was pleased with the results. His business grew rapidly as word spread about his quality work, and appointments became increasingly difficult to secure.

Some months later, I returned to have my car serviced again. To an outside observer, he clearly needed to do things differently. Everywhere, cars awaited servicing. Jammed in the tiny garage were four cars in a space normally occupied by two. Rows of cars sat two abreast in the driveway, while others, awaiting his masterful attention, surrounded the small station.

Within months, an announcement that he had a new location arrived in the mail. He had leased a small warehouse to serve as his garage, and it had much more room. I laughed when I saw his "new" situation. Cars jammed the larger quarters. Others, waiting for servicing, lined up *four* abreast in the driveway while additional cars surrounded the warehouse. He had changed his address but had maintained the same situation!

Instead of changing addresses, address the issue.

How many times have we "changed addresses," only to discover that all the "stuff" from our past has followed us into our new situation? A woman married to an alcoholic husband finally decides that she's had enough. After divorcing and eventually remarrying, she discovers that her "new" husband is another alcoholic. A man, discouraged with the lack of recognition he receives in his current job, leaves in pursuit of better circumstances. Within months, he experiences the same lack of appreciation on the "new" job. A teenager, involved with the wrong crowd, switches schools to get a fresh start. You can guess the results. A new school, yet the "same" old gang.

Rodney Dangerfield, the comedian, says, "I don't get no respect." No matter where he goes, audiences behave the same way—not "respecting" him. While his act has made him rich and famous, our own act may not have the same results. We often drag along the same old patterns from the past and duplicate them in new locations and new relationships. Letting our old patterns run the show positions us to experience the same outcomes.

Rarely will changing our circumstances address the issues. In fact, it may only postpone the inner work calling for attention. All meaningful change comes from the inside, not from our external circumstances. Inner work has to do with confronting and working through the context or internal issues. Rearranging the circumstances or external issues consumes time and resources, yet does not deal with the chronic, underlying causes. We can keep busy rearranging the deck chairs on the sinking *Titanic,* but this ignores the obvious problem.

By working on ourselves rather than our circumstances, we enhance our effectiveness and therefore positively influence the conditions in which we find ourselves. Rather than consuming energy and resources to escape or attack our circumstances, we achieve better results by going directly into the areas we resist. The way out is *through!*

Circumstances do not determine who you are or what you do; instead, they reveal your inner being. When you choose to respond with conscious awareness, you not only materially influence your surrounding circumstances, but enhance your results as well.

"Problems are sent to us as gifts."

Ancient Oriental teaching

Problems are sent to us as gifts, and some of us have many gifts! The same problem will return again and again until we get the learning. When we move outside of our awareness, we may even seek out problems as a path to discovery. Once we pause, seek out the learning, and behaviorally apply what we learn, the problem need not return. Even though the learning itself can be painful, consciously seeking the learning positions us to make a positive difference in our life. Experiencing short-term pain for long-term gain is often part of the learning and growing process.

Ignoring your "stuff" positions you to deal with the circumstances rather than the actual issue. That which you resist persists and often intensifies. Imagine an elephant in your living room knocking over lamps, making "deposits" on the carpet, and bumping into walls. Now imagine family members sitting in the living room and pretending to ignore the elephant's presence. Everyone knows about the elephant and experiences its consequences, yet no one willingly acknowledges the reality of its existence. By denying the issues that call for our attention, we commit to maintaining the status quo. And the circumstances frequently continue to worsen. Is it possible that there's an elephant in your "living room"?

"As our case is new, we must think and act anew."

Abraham Lincoln

Recall the classic biology experiment—the boiled frog syndrome. The experiment begins with a frog in a pot of cold water. As the water gradually heats up, the frog chooses to remain and slowly boils to death. The slight increases in temperature go unnoticed until it is too late to take action.

Many hospitals, banks, insurance companies, churches, universities, steel companies, and automobile manufacturers as well as individuals are like the frog. They don't wake up until the world has passed them by. The competitive environment continues to heat up, and they continue to sleep and maintain their comfort zone. Churches and temples "suddenly" find their pews empty. U.S. automobile manufacturers "discover" that a large percentage of their market share has been lost to foreign cars. Bankers arrive at 9:30 on Monday morning only to find their front doors padlocked by federal authorities. And individuals wonder why they are passed over—the third time—for promotion. Wake-up calls. Boiled frogs.

"It stopped being fun here sixteen years ago" reported an executive to me during an organizational assessment interview. He was forty-two years old and waiting to retire! Retire? He had already retired on the job. I guess he gets paid for just showing up. No passion. No creativity. Lots of reasons. Lots of excuses. He allowed the situation to worsen until his spirit died. Early on he settled for the unacceptable, became numb, and allowed circumstances to determine his destiny.

Why would anyone want to stay in a job that is unsatisfying? Life is too short. If you don't love your work enough to excel, cautions Brian Tracy, then "flee that unsatisfying job as you would a burning building." Why waste your life on something that drains energy? So many other options exist. I know you think you have reasons for staying. When you argue for your limitations, however, all you get are your limitations. By settling for less than the best, you create that very result in your life. As the late Reverend Jack Boland said, "Good is the enemy of the best!"

What if you offered to a four-year-old child the choice of one ice cream scoop today or two scoops tomorrow? The child will take one scoop today—every time. Offer the same choice to an adult and the response differs: "I'm no fool. If I wait until tomorrow, I'll get two scoops!" So the adult postpones gratification until the next day. Think of people you know who said, "I'm going to start living when I retire," and then died within months of their retirement. Boiled frogs.

When we are willing to examine our hurts, fears, and dysfunctions, healing begins. A significant majority of the time, the answers to dealing with our issues are within. We already know what we need to know and have the resources to deal with our stuff. Instead, we often allow ourselves to get caught in a stuck state and repeat patterns that do not work. These patterns intrude into the present and make out of the present—the past.

Destructive or counterproductive patterns are recycled at our "new address," even though a part of us knows that what we are doing does not work! Learning to pause and tap into our existing internal resources, on the other hand, enables us to take **69** charge of our lives and position ourselves to learn, grow, and make a positive difference.

On relatively rare occasions, you may not have the answers or internal resources to deal with your own issues. A wise person acknowledges these limits and seeks outside resources to help in addressing the inner work that requires attention. While no one can do your life's work for you, skilled professionals can assist in punching through barriers, holding you accountable, providing options, and encouraging you to experience life at a more fulfilling level. Because you cannot escape your life issues, why not transform them?

Be cautious about the external "resources" you call upon to assist you in doing your work. When you are not feeling whole and complete, the temptation exists to fill the emptiness with drugs, alcohol, or dysfunctional people. Addiction or co-dependency can result—and the hole gets bigger. As Ian McIver said at a seminar: "When you are in a hole, stop digging."

Each challenge we face contains an opportunity that is usually far greater than the problem itself. Often, the situation itself may prepare us to deal with far greater future demands on our talents. When we focus on the obstacle, we miss the opportunity. The greatest successes in life occur when we convert an obstacle into an opportunity. The learning tends to stick and our self-esteem ultimately advances when we address the issues that need attention.

"The past does not equal the future."

Anthony Robbins

While the past influences your future, it certainly does not control it—unless you consent! You may not be responsible for your past, yet you are in charge of your future. The choices you make today shape the future and also potentially influence your life circumstances. It has been said: "We cannot direct the wind—but we can adjust the sails."

AWARENESS CHECKS

- What in your life are you unwilling to face?

- Instead of dealing with the inner work calling for attention, are you attempting to change the external circumstances?

- Are you allowing the unacceptable to slowly kill your spirit?

- Are you changing addresses only to discover the same old stuff?

- What is the learning right now?

Instead of changing addresses, address the issue. The way out is through.

7

Sleepwalking Versus Awakening:
MOVING TOWARD GREATER AWARENESS

"I am awake."

The Buddha

No instruction manuals were provided as we entered into our life experience. Confronted with this situation, we have two choices for learning what we need to learn. One involves tapping into our internal resources and the other requires learning from external sources. An immediate dilemma arises. Often our internal resources have not been well enough developed to effectively carry us through life situations. And we make lots of mistakes. External sources (parents, friends, spouses) also may not be as awake as they need to be, so at times relying on their perceptions and advice doesn't work well either. And we make lots of mistakes.

By consciously choosing to increase our awareness, however, we can use both our internal and external resources far more effectively. Yes, awareness itself is a choice. Awareness involves getting straight with ourselves and our environment so that we can make better life choices. The more aware we are, the more choices we have. The less aware, the fewer choices.

Some people choose to sleepwalk through relationships, careers, and other life experiences. Learning is missed as old patterns repeat. The same issues keep coming up over and over again—and we wonder why these things "keep happening to us." Rather than pausing to absorb the learning, we focus on rationalizing, justifying, defending, and saving face. The resulting stuck state consumes enormous energy while blocking learning opportunities.

> ## *"What concerns me is not the way things are, but rather the way people think things are."*
>
> Epictetus

You are influenced more by what you *think* is so than what actually *is* so. Your perceptions of reality do more to govern your behavior than reality itself. When you learn to pay attention, you create an opportunity to switch from passive to active awareness.

As a demonstration of your awareness and perceptions, examine the awareness checks in the accompanying illustration and answer the following questions:

1. In quadrant A, how many squares do you see?

2. In quadrant B, what do you read within the triangle?

3. In quadrant C, how many "F's" do you see?

4. In quadrant D, what do you see?

AWARENESS CHECKS

A. HOW MANY SQUARES?

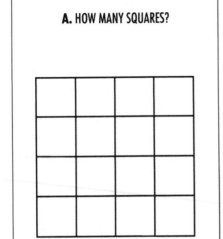

B. WHAT DO YOU READ?

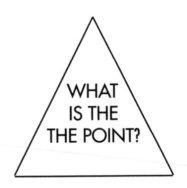

WHAT
IS THE
THE POINT?

C. FIND THE "F's"

FIGHTING FIRE FIGHTERS
ARE THE PRODUCT OF
YEARS OF CAREFUL
TRAINING COMBINED
WITH YEARS OF
ON-THE-JOB EXPERIENCE.

D. WHAT DO YOU SEE?

Just because we experience the world in a certain form does not mean that the world actually exists that way. Perceptions form the basis of our opinions, our position in an argument, the quality of our relationships, our feelings, and even our quality of life. Paying attention to perceptions and awareness levels is instrumental in making a positive life difference for us and those around us. As we advance from a sleepwalking to an awakened state, we feel fear, excitement, and eventually genuine fulfillment. By experiencing things differently, we tend to think, feel, and do things differently. The journey into higher awareness can become more important than the destination. Let's examine further how perceptions are formed.

In quadrant A, most people quickly scan the diagram and identify either sixteen or seventeen squares. Both answers are correct! Sixteen one-by-one-inch squares exist. Yet a seventeenth—the large one—forms the outer perimeter. To the more careful observer, however, a total of thirty are formed by the additional nine two-by-two-inch squares and four three-by-three-inch squares.

When presented with the thirty-square awareness check, most people focus on the diagram, quickly conclude that sixteen or seventeen squares exist, and stop their creative process! Ever since childhood, we have been trained to look for "one right answer." Our schoolteachers taught us that a question is either true or false, or that a multiple-choice question has only one "right" answer. When we continue to seek this "one right answer" in other life experiences, we miss many other options.

Consider the individual who must always be right. She will lock on to the sixteen-square position and lock out the other fourteen. She is unwilling to consider other options, even as others attempt to share a different perspective. Rather than listening, however, she prepares her rebuttal as she waits to talk. Unwilling to move off her position and be open to influence, she limits her awareness.

As the story goes, Albert Einstein flunked out of school because he was not in sync with his teachers. If he were to be asked by the teacher how many squares he saw, Albert's likely response would have been "Thirty!" Seeing only sixteen, the teacher would have said, "Albert, you are wrong—again." Einstein experienced the world differently from his instructors, and because his views differed, his teachers continually marked him down. How many times do we consider a different perspective to be "wrong"? How many times do we "mark others down" for doing or perceiving things differently?

In quadrant B, you might read, "What is the point?" That seems simple enough, but it is not what it says. Reread the question within the triangle, perhaps starting from the last word forward. Do you see anything differently? Usually fewer than 10 percent of readers will be aware of the actual question: "What is the *the* point?" "The" appears twice, yet most people do not see the duplication. Our experience of reality seems accurate, yet this diagram again challenges that assumption. Examine times when you and an important person in your life viewed something differently. Convinced of your own perspective, each of you sleepwalked through another life event.

In quadrant C, finding the "F's" becomes the challenge. Look closely and count carefully. Some will find three, others five, and a rare few will find nine! How many did you discover in your perception check? Those who find four are only looking at the body of the sentence and are ignoring the quadrant title, which contains two more. Those who find nine see two in the title and seven in the sentence itself. If you are still struggling, count the word "of." Three more "F's" now jump out of the page. Missing the letter "F" in the word "of" is common.

We have a blind spot that often makes us miss things that are present. It is no wonder that disagreements between individuals occur as each relies on his or her own perceptions of reality while locking out other options. Just because the world is experienced in a certain way does not mean that it actually *is* that way.

Another interesting observation about this phenomenon relates to diversity of perceptions. When we show the "nine F's" and "thirty squares" to groups of people, individuals invariably come to different conclusions, even when they are presented with the same information at the same time. Diverse perceptions **77** can both enrich relationships and contribute to interpersonal discord.

Experience results from our perceptions, which are filtered through such factors as our history, culture, values, desire, education, and awareness. Given our perceptions and filtering system, we begin to have a clearer understanding of why people struggle with understanding reality. Interpersonal and organizational strife frequently result from perceptual differences. Understanding this dilemma helps us to develop more empathy for the position of others.

Quadrant D presents the toughest challenge for most people, who focus on the black objects and miss the white space in between. Does this clue help? If not, rotate the book clockwise one-quarter turn and focus on the *white* space between the black objects. Perhaps you can now see the word "FLY" in large, white block letters.

Changing perspective, or viewing the diagram from a different view, enables us to discover something that now appears strikingly obvious. Called "reframing," this intentional process of viewing the same situation from different perspectives can be a powerful tool for enhancing awareness. Life experiences, whether at work or home, present many reframing opportunities. When we are open to the learning, willing to move off our position, and receptive to viewing things from a different perspective, we can discover a whole new world. What might you discover from reframing?

"The significant problems we face cannot be resolved at the same level of thinking we were at when we created them."

Albert Einstein

Some recent lessons in history underscore this principle. Recall when former president Ronald Reagan referred to the Soviet Union as the "Evil Empire." His first summit meeting with Soviet General Secretary Mikhail Gorbachev was unproductive and seemed only to reinforce his previously held bias. At their December 1987 meeting in Washington, D.C., however, the two leaders *listened* to one another and discovered mutual interests. They each changed perspective, and the world became a safer place.

Following the meeting, General Secretary Gorbachev expressed to the international press corps his belief that both countries must now struggle against "long-held emotions and stereotypes." President Reagan followed by stating: "We've proven that adversaries, even with the most basic philosophical differences, can talk candidly and respectfully with one another, and with perseverance, find common ground." Being open to a different viewpoint and being on listening terms creates miracles both interpersonally and internationally. The rapid demise of the Soviet Union and Communism clearly demonstrates the catalytic power of awareness in facilitating change—transformational change.

The more aware we are, the more choices we have. The less aware we are, the fewer choices. Sometimes people claim: "I have no choice." In taking this position, awareness levels and behavioral options are limited. We *always* have a choice, even though we may not like the *consequences* of the choice. We do not have to pay taxes, for example, yet the consequences of not paying them are significant.

Awareness of the world around us is likened to tuning in to a radio station. At any given time, scores of radio waves bombard our unconscious environment. Until we turn on our radio receiver, however, the messages go undetected. Even at that point, tuning in to one station causes us to miss others. This metaphor applies to our relationship, career, and other life realities. We receive life messages only on the frequencies to which we are tuned. And even those messages filter through our sensory limitations.

Helen Keller, one of the more astute teachers in recent times, could have found it easy to sleepwalk through life. Blind

79

and deaf, she had difficulty both sending and receiving messages. Yet she had the desire to connect with the world, to be a meaningful part of it, and not to allow her "limitations" to limit her. To receive messages from our inner and outer worlds, we need to (1) have the receiving equipment, (2) turn it on, and (3) tune in. We have the equipment. Turning on the receiver and tuning in are choice points that assist us in moving from sleepwalking to awakening.

"The way we see the problem is the problem."

Stephen R. Covey

Our "reality" consists of three parts: awareness, deletions, and distortions. Reality is defined simply as "what is." Tuning in to reality is a process of becoming more aware. The more our map of reality matches what is, the more in tune we are with our inner and outer world. In illustrating this process, we can represent reality by the shaded portion. The dotted line symbolizes "my" reality. It is hoped that some overlap exists between reality and "my" reality! The overlap represents a state of *awareness*, where my map of reality matches what is. The greater the overlap, the greater the awareness.

Sometimes we compartmentalize our awareness. In some areas of our life, a healthy overlap exists between reality and our own perception of reality. In other areas, however, we can be out of touch. A police officer, for example, might be tuned in to danger signals while working in an area with a high crime rate, yet be unaware of a developing drug addiction problem with his own teenager. A corporate executive might be highly astute in making sensitive and timely decisions but may sleepwalk through her relationship at home. Where are you compartmentalizing your awareness? In which parts of your life are you in tune and where might you benefit by expanding your awareness?

80

REALITY: What *is.*

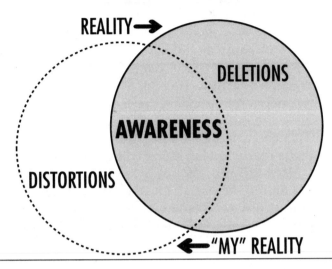

Deletions are those parts of "what is" that we simply do not experience. When we tune in to a particular frequency, other radio stations seeking our attention go by unnoticed. In the awareness checks in the early part of this chapter, perhaps you saw only sixteen squares where there were thirty. Or you did not see the second "the" in "What is the the point?" Looking for the "F's," you may have discovered five when there were nine. Just because we do not experience something does not mean that it does not exist. Our filtering system can delete important information and feelings, and we end up "numbing out" in our life and relationships.

Distortions are not a part of reality, yet we think they are! And we feel so strongly that we act on these distortions. We often make assumptions about what others think, feel, and want, and we determine our decisions and actions based on these assumptions. If we assume that someone does not like us, we act accordingly. Relations with in-laws, stepchildren, and bosses are often laced with distortions, as are those with our spouse or partner.

The "horn-halo" effect we learned in Psychology 101 addresses distortions. Those we label as having "horns" can do **81** no right. Those labeled as having "halos" can do no wrong from our distorted perspective.

Deletions and distortions compete with awareness. Our lifelong challenge is to enhance our awareness levels to the point where our map of reality matches what is. The process of awakening, of learning, and of discovering becomes an important part of life's journey. How, then, do we increase our awareness? At the risk of oversimplifying, there are two strategies for awakening: the *traumatic* and the *conscious.*

Some of us need a significant emotional event or wake-up call to even get us ready to view things differently. A divorce, a major illness, getting fired, losing a key client, flunking an important examination—these are the more traumatic methods of attracting our attention. These can be life's way of sending "gifts" for learning, growing, and self-correcting. Painful as it may be, a significant emotional event can be the catalyst for choosing a direction that serves us—and those around us—more effectively. Look for the learning.

Conscious awakening, on the other hand, becomes a choice to increase our awareness. Your choice to read this book is evidence of your conscious effort to expand awareness. A conscious commitment to increasing awareness can create even more effective life results when the following awareness strategies are practiced:

Awareness Strategies

Remaining Unaware	*vs.*	*Increasing Awareness*
Maintaining my position	vs.	Moving off my position
Talking	vs.	Listening
Maintaining my comfort zone	vs.	Being willing to risk
Maintaining my territory	vs.	Exploring new hunting grounds
Defending an old position	vs.	Exploring new ideas
Being "right"	vs.	Asking "What if . . . ?"

Protecting	vs.	Being vulnerable
Withholding	vs.	Sharing
Repeating behaviors	vs.	Experimenting with new behaviors
Blocking feedback	vs.	Encouraging feedback
Blaming	vs.	Looking inward
"Why is this happening to me?"	vs.	"What is the learning?"
Pretending not to know	vs.	Asking
Pretending to know	vs.	Seeking clarification
Assuming	vs.	Inquiring
Reacting	vs.	Pausing

Which of these patterns do you practice? What results do you achieve?

Moving off your position can become one of your more powerful awareness strategies, particularly when it is combined with listening. Where in your life might you experience only "sixteen squares." If you maintain this position and block feedback, no amount of convincing will succeed in demonstrating a different perspective to you. The sixteen-square position might be altered, however, if you instead paused, said "Tell me more," and listened. Such receptivity to feedback might then successfully reveal the thirty squares. Where might you be coming to premature closure? Where might you be unwilling to move off your position? Where might you benefit by consciously practicing the awareness strategies?

"*Is there life* before *death?*"

Alan Cohen

The diagram of the Triple-A Strategy illustrates three steps in making a difference: *awareness, action,* and *actualization.* Each interdependent element facilitates the

83

MAKING A DIFFERENCE:
The Triple-A Strategy

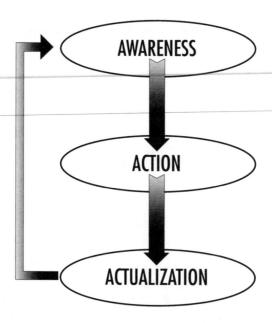

change process. Although people do the very best they can, given their level of awareness, that awareness is neutralized without action. We all know of aware people who talk the talk, yet don't walk the talk. Awareness is an essential first step, but it becomes useful only when it is put into action, using tangible, specific behavioral steps. Ask: "What can I do right now that will make a positive difference?"

Actualization is a manifestation of the action phase. Life outcomes, whether they are effective or ineffective, provide additional learning opportunities. By pausing to evaluate results, we increase awareness and therefore position ourselves to produce even better results. And the cycle repeats.

Application of the Triple-A Strategy results from a conscious commitment to growth and renewal. This self-empowerment process represents an important step in moving from a sleepwalking to an awakened state—from fizzle to sizzle!

Alan Cohen, a friend and author, refers to people who have had a near-death experience. Considerable interest has been focused on studying these encounters and thousands of cases have been documented. Cohen, on the other hand, playfully considered establishing a research institute to study those who have had *near-life* experiences. Among those who could be suitable research subjects are the walking dead, those who have "numbed out," mere "survivors," those who have postponed life, the sleepwalkers, couch potatoes, and those who have engaged their snooze alarms rather than being open to a wake-up call. Just because you engage in activity doesn't mean you are alive. Cohen challenges: "Is there life *before* death?"

Awareness is a choice.

Some of us play hooky from life school and end up sleepwalking through relationships, careers, and important life moments. We can be unaware and even closed to life's teachers and teachings. In this stuck-state cycle, we may miss the joy and fulfillment of life. Under these circumstances, we are ripe for receiving significant wake-up calls, in which we have an opportunity to switch from passive to active awareness; without action, awareness is neutralized. Part of our lifelong challenge involves converting what we already know into results that serve us and others at a higher level. The life process is not about perfection. It is about self-awareness and self-correction.

Past choices influence yet do not control our destiny. Decisions we make today do more to shape our future than those made yesterday. Wake-up calls abound. Choose life over sleepwalking. Commit to converting your teachable moments into positive life results. Commit to taking charge of your life at an even higher level.

AWARENESS CHECKS

- Where in your life are you sleepwalking?

- Where might you make a positive difference by allowing yourself to be more aware and to take action?

- How are you blocking your growth?

- Where do you need healing—mentally, physically, spiritually, emotionally?

- Where would forgiveness provide healing, either within yourself or between yourself and someone else?

- Where do you feel stuck or incomplete?

- What do you need to let go of in order to have peace?

- What talents and skills do you want to acquire or develop?

- How can you create more joy and fulfillment in your life?

- What is trying to happen in your life?

- What is your next step for growth?

- What is the learning here?

Part 2

TAKING
CHARGE

CHAPTER

Accountability:
SHAPE OR BE SHAPED!

**"I will not surrender responsibility
for my life and my actions."**

John Powell

Woody Allen once said, "Eighty percent of success is just showing up." Actually, 80 percent of *life* is just showing up. Some of us show up just 80 percent of the time, some 90 percent, and some 100 percent! How fully do you show up?

How many of you have said to yourself when you were invited to a party, "I hope it's going to be a good party!" Be honest. When you say this, where are you placing the responsibility for making it a good party? Obviously, on everyone else. And what if they turn out to be the kind of party goers you don't enjoy being with? You can count on it being a lousy party.

Another way of going to a party is to commit to yourself and say, "It's going to be a good party because *I'm going to be there!*" Where are you placing the responsibility for making it a good party this time? On yourself. And that's what you can count on the most. When you take accountability for creating your own results, you are much more likely to have a fulfilling experience.

Accountability claims your own power and uses your own resources to create even better results in life. It asks you to go into new situations with a conscious focus on what you can do right now that will make a positive difference. Through accountability, you take charge of your thoughts, feelings, and actions regardless of what the other "party goers" do and create your own reality through a sequence of life choices.

Practicing accountability as a critical life strategy makes a positive difference. In my research of peak-performing individuals and organizations, I have found that integrating the spirit of accountability into daily thinking and behaviors becomes a fundamental factor in experiencing life at a higher level. These people take charge of their life and look inward, not outward, for results. They claim responsibility for both their successes and their "failures." These individuals are not an effect; they are the cause.

All meaningful change comes from within.

People who live with conscious accountability are not immune to tough life experiences. Like any of us, they have peaks and valleys in their life process. Conscious accountability does, however, significantly reduce their conflict, trauma, "accidents," and victimization.

Conscious accountability empowers your *internal* resources to be of service in experiencing life at a more fulfilling level. Internal resources, especially when they are nurtured, frequently have more power than outside forces. Self-development positions you to respond effectively to a window of opportunity. Empowering *external* forces, on the other hand, turns your power and control over to other circumstances and people—to let them pull your strings like a puppet.

Rather than accept accountability, many people say, "Fix my relationships. Fix my boss. Fix my career. Fix my finances. Fix my health. Fix my life. But don't mess with my mind. Don't make me look inward. Don't make me be accountable." If you don't take charge of shaping your own destiny, others will apply their agenda to you.

Consider these two options in dealing with a tough life experience:

1. *Nonaccountable behaviors:* "Why do these things always happen to me?" or "Who is to blame for this situation?"

2. *Accountable behaviors:* "What is the learning for me?" or "What can I do to make a positive difference?"

Note how differently the mind processes these two approaches. The first question erodes our esteem or the esteem of others. As long as we blame ourselves or others, we miss the learning. Shifting the responsibility elsewhere or becoming immobilized by self-blame keeps us in a stuck state. We remain ignorant of our contribution to the situation and are likely to reexperience the same result in the future.

The more accountable option allows our mind to creatively explore the learning options, and we grow in the process. For example, almost every time I have been criticized, even "unjustly," important learning awaits me. Usually a gem is waiting to be discovered if I am willing to become quiet inside and seek the learning.

Bring to mind a situation in your life when you were a victim, when you felt used, taken advantage of, or treated unfairly in some way. What specific feelings did you experience about the other person? About yourself? Reflect on this for a moment.

Now for the stretch. Be willing to experiment by reframing the event. Look at that same situation very differently—from a

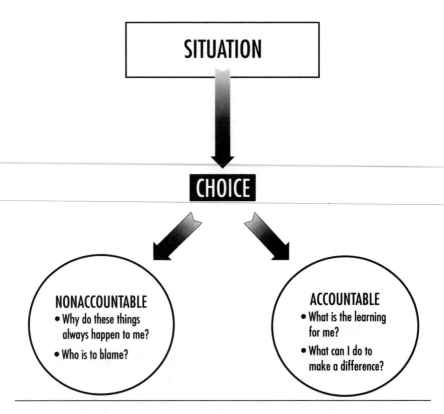

100 percent accountable point of view! (Not just 50 percent of the accountability. This sets you up to be a victim half of the time. Be willing to accept 100 percent of the accountability for your thoughts, feelings, and behaviors.) How might *you* have set it up to experience those results? How do you feel about your sense of power, control, self-esteem, and dignity, given that situation? What might you have said or done differently to create a more positive outcome?

"No one can hurt you without your consent."

Eleanor Roosevelt

LET ME SHARE ONE OF MY past victim stories. When I was a hospital administrator some years ago, I was confronted with a community problem concerning how to treat "police hold" cases. These consisted of individuals who were thought by the police to be dangerous to themselves or others— psychiatric emergencies. After detaining these people, police dropped them off at the hospital's emergency department. Emergency medicine physicians, however, seemed to be more interested in fractures and lacerations than psychiatric crises. Patients were usually referred to an "on-call" psychiatrist, frequently in the middle of the night, for their treatment. Psychiatrists didn't want to get out of bed to treat a person who would entangle them with legal problems and who usually could not afford to pay for their care. Admitting these patients to the hospital in the custody of nurses was inappropriate, as the patients were sometimes dangerous and destructive. Jailing them was not a good option, for they usually were not criminals. The courts did not know what to do with them either, as they fell into neither the criminal justice nor medical systems.

Efforts to resolve the situation were unsuccessful, and the whole system of caring for these unique patients collapsed. The news media had a field day. The entire health-care community and the criminal justice system were on public trial. Patients were the biggest losers, however, as agencies and professionals directed their energy to fixing blame rather than fixing the problem.

Under these conditions, I traveled to a number of communities to study how they successfully handled "police hold" cases. Armed with a number of viable options, I returned to my own community and organized problem-solving efforts. One political figure in the community was in a pivotal position. His support or opposition would determine the outcome. I made an appointment with him, *enthusiastically* shared the new ideas, and asked for his support. He said, "Let's go for it."

Having attained his support, I then went on to the hospital board of directors, the county commissioners, and other key people to secure a united front. All systems were "go," or so I thought. Behind my back, however, the politician sabotaged the program. As it turned out, he didn't like the original idea, but he didn't have the guts to tell me directly. The whole process came to a halt. The news media renewed its relentless attacks. Although

93

the politician succeeded in sidetracking the process temporarily, we later resolved the issue in a slightly different form.

I felt like a victim of this politician's self-serving tactics. How could he do this to me? How could he be so divisive and underhanded? I felt used, abused, and treated unfairly. I was steamed!

Let's create another scenario and examine this situation from an *accountable* point of view. As long as I focused on the factors outside of myself, I missed the learning. Clearly, I am responsible for *my* thoughts, feelings, and behaviors. And the politician was responsible for *his* thoughts, feelings, and behaviors.

How did I set the situation up to experience the results I achieved? What could I have said or done differently to have produced a more effective outcome? Saying that I "enthusiastically" shared my ideas with the politician was an understatement. I came into his office like a bulldozer, and I wanted his support *now*. I knew him to be highly analytical. He needed process time—thinking time to sort through alternatives. If I had chosen to be more aware and accountable, I would have shared the alternatives with him, asked him to think about the options, and requested that he explore the ideas with other people. Then we could have gotten together a week later to discuss his perspective. Clearly, together we could have developed a more politically acceptable solution, saved an enormous amount of time, and come away feeling better about ourselves.

Just 20/20 hindsight, you say? Not at all. Living with accountability in new situations involves choosing to be more aware, using available resources at a higher level, and making the head-heart connection—in effect, *choosing to make a positive difference.* The results, personally and professionally, are rewarding.

Even though most people want to be accountable, they sometimes get caught up in the emotion of a situation and lose the learning. Consider reviewing one of your own victim stories from a 100 percent accountable perspective. How do you feel about your sense of power, self-esteem, control, self-worth? Reframing how you view a nonaccountable time in your life can be a breakthrough moment. The chances are that you will feel

94

young man, he felt on top of the world. Having soloed an airplane for the first time, he was particularly proud. Later that day, he climbed on his new motorcycle and drove through the streets of San Francisco. A laundry truck ran a stop sign and the two collided. The truck won. In addition to fractures, Mitchell's most serious problems resulted when the motorcycle's gas tank exploded, spilling flaming fuel over his entire body. His face was nearly burned off.

After many operations and two years of medical recovery, he went on with his life, even though he was now ugly and disfigured. He told the following story:

> During the next two years in San Francisco, I forgot how unacceptable I was. I forgot that there was anything wrong with me. I forgot that I was ugly. And you know, other people did too. You see, what I learned during those two years that it took me to fully recover—to learn to dress myself again, to drive again, and, yes, even to fly an airplane again—was that what I focus on in life is what I get. And if I concentrate on how bad I am or how wrong I am or how inadequate I am, if I concentrate on what I can't do and how there's not enough time in which to do it, isn't that what I get every time? And when I think about how powerful I am, and when I think about what I have left to contribute, and when I think about the difference that I can make on this planet, then that's what I get. You see, I recognize that it's not what happens to you; it's what you do about it.

W. Mitchell is a giant of a man—and an important teacher. Yet his story does not end there. His love of flying beckoned. Some years later, another major accident, this time in his airplane. Mitchell's legs were now permanently paralyzed. While he was in the hospital and learning to use his new wheelchair, he met a young man who was not doing well. This former athlete's world ended when he lost the use of his legs. Confined to a wheelchair, he could no longer ski and climb mountains. Mitchell decided to talk with his fellow patient:

> One day, after trying the best I could to think of something to say that could help him that might make a difference, I

97

went over to him. I told him that before I was paralyzed, there were ten thousand things that I could do. Now there are nine thousand. Sure, I could dwell on the thousand that I lost, if that's how I chose to spend the rest of my life. Or I could focus on the nine thousand that I have left. And if, in my lifetime, I'm able to do even a few hundred of those things, I'll be one of the most remarkable people on this planet. You see, its not what happens to you; it's what you do about it that makes the difference.

W. Mitchell lives his life as a beginner. He looks for the learning. He went on to become mayor of Crested Butte, Colorado. In 1984, he ran for Congress. Although the other person received more votes, Mitchell experienced yet another win in his life. He learned more about himself and came out an even better person for the experience. He philosophized: "The only losers are the people who don't get into the race. The only losers are the people who don't stand up to be counted. The only losers are the people who don't try to make a difference." Mitchell's accountability in taking charge of his life under the most extreme circumstances presents an inspirational role model. Clearly, he shapes his own destiny.

"All the water in the world cannot drown you—unless it gets inside."

Mary Manin Boggs

Practicing accountability as a fundamental life strategy enables us to experience life at a more fulfilling level. Integrating the spirit of accountability into daily thinking and behaviors becomes the difference that makes a difference. We are not an effect; we are the cause.

Getting your life to hum starts from within. Shape or be shaped—the choice is yours. And now is the time.

AWARENESS CHECKS

- Where are you choosing to be a victim?

- How does this block you from growing?

- What are the current costs of choosing to be victimized?

- How would your life work better if you re-created a more accountable history?

- What are you willing to do differently to create more positive outcomes in your life?

- What is the learning here?

Pause Power:
CONNECTING HEAD
AND HEART

*"What lies behind us
and what lies before us
are tiny matters compared to
what lies within us."*

Oliver Wendell Holmes

An important teacher once said to me: "The longest journey in life is only eighteen inches—connecting the head with the heart." The head and heart, figuratively speaking, are our two most important and useful internal resources. Consciously developing *and connecting* these two dimensions enables us to enhance our competence (head) and our ability to love and be loved (heart). Life is experienced at a much more fulfilling level when we use these two internal resources to their maximum, but in many of us, they are often disconnected, causing us to miss or misinterpret much of what happens around us. Under these conditions, we are more likely to receive a wake-up call "out of the blue."

Those of us who live in our heads tend to interpret the world through an objective filter. We look at things logically, systematically, and rationally. This black-and-white left-brain world is tangible, or so we think. What we focus on determines what we miss. And how much we miss through this myopic view!

Those of us who live in our hearts view the world through a subjective filter. We experience life events as more intangible. Feelings, intuition, and our "inner voice" become more important. This right-brain approach values judgment and interpretation. And what we focus on still determines what we miss.

What we focus on determines what we miss—and what we become!

Both the head and the heart are important internal resources in dealing with life issues. Neither can be ignored if we wish to experience life at its fullest. Both dimensions are required to achieve balance; they are like having an internal board of directors at our disposal to guide us through life issues and decisions.

Access to the combined resources of the head and heart is achieved through *pausing*. Not merely a time intermission, pausing is a conscious process of becoming quiet inside and listening to the counsel of our internal board of directors. This process momentarily locks out external stimuli and internal self-talk to permit us to connect the head with the heart.

If we are new to this process, we might view the initial results as superficial and inconsequential. With conscious persistence and practice, however, the results can be profound. Most of us are familiar with the fact that we tend to use less than 10 percent of our brain's capacity. Pausing with intent enables us to access the untapped reserves of our brain and put them into service. The process of consciously pausing literally develops more physiological connectors between the left and right parts of the brain, resulting in even easier access to our untapped potential with continued practice.

Life reflects the sum total of our choices. Sometimes we become locked into a short-term pattern of reacting to immediate needs and missing the longer-term benefits of positioning ourselves to deal with more important life issues and priorities. Through conscious self-examination, more options are created. Since we are a product of our choices, pausing periodically to examine our mission, priorities, fulfillment level, and results becomes an important life assessment process. We cannot ignore these choices; either we will make the decisions or they will be made for us.

The head-heart connection applies to organizations as well as to individuals. For a dozen years, I have studied peak-performing organizations to discover what principles and practices they apply to achieve such favorable long-term results. Their corporate commitment to excellence clearly balances both the bottom line and the human element. Less-than-effective organizations pay lip service to maintaining balance, while those with a long-term track record of excellence commit to their values through tangible practices and behaviors.

Out-of-balance organizations may emphasize the bottom line and productivity at the expense of the human element. As a result of their "sweat shop" conditions, turnover and absenteeism accelerate. Individuals keep their résumés polished and seek opportunities elsewhere. Risk taking seems unsafe and the stressful environment stifles creativity, as employees direct significant attention to protecting themselves rather then serving the organization and its clients. Employees feel used and abused, and they frequently depend on unions to assist in meeting their unfilled needs. Eventually even profits and productivity suffer. These organizations "kill the goose that laid the golden eggs." They focus on the head and miss the heart.

Other organizations focus on the human element and miss the bottom line. Although employees may temporarily feel good about this type of organization, lack of attention to profits and **103** productivity eventually results in serious problems and perhaps even bankruptcy, and dissatisfaction creeps into the organization. People need to believe they are making a meaningful contribution, and these organizations do not achieve challenging levels of personal fulfillment. So much attention is focused on "taking care of the goose" that collecting the golden eggs becomes a secondary priority. They focus on the heart and miss the head.

Some organizations focus on neither the bottom line nor the human element. Not only are they out of balance, but they have no concept of mission, purpose, client service, or self-esteem. Like "walking dead," individuals in these companies focus on survival, risk avoidance, self-protection, and retirement. Having lost their direction and spirit, they say, "What goose? What eggs?"

Peak-performing organizations commit to balancing the head and the heart. Even in tight financial times, they often invest in their people to provide every opportunity for success. They balance the bottom line (the head) with the human element (the heart). This corporate commitment to excellence permeates the entire organization. While they are not perfect, they self-correct when they become out of balance. Hewitt Associates, Les Schwab Tire Service, Delta Air Lines, Nordstrom, Alaska Airlines, Disneyland, Compri Hotel, IBM, and others are noted for their commitment to a balanced environment. They also have the courage to make corporate adjustments when appropriate to maintain balance. They practice "taking care of the goose—and receiving the golden eggs."

Listen to and develop your inner guidance.

Most people talk about wanting to live a balanced life, yet few actually do well applying this concept. As we focus on one area of our life, another part eventually reminds us of its need for attention. When we are out of balance, the likelihood of receiving a wake-up call significantly increases. By focusing on our career, for example, we are more likely to miss

LIFE BALANCE

	Balance Ranking					
Heart-Focused	1	2	3	2	1	Head-Focused
			(Balanced)			
Being	1	2	3	2	1	Doing
Spiritual	1	2	3	2	1	Physical
Worthiness	1	2	3	2	1	Competence
People	1	2	3	2	1	Productivity
Lovable	1	2	3	2	1	Capable
Intention	1	2	3	2	1	Action
Leisure	1	2	3	2	1	Work
Attitude	1	2	3	2	1	Ability
Right brain	1	2	3	2	1	Left brain
Intuition	1	2	3	2	1	Intelligence
Others	1	2	3	2	1	Self
Family	1	2	3	2	1	Career
Creativity	1	2	3	2	1	Logic
Giving	1	2	3	2	1	Receiving
Human element	1	2	3	2	1	Bottom line

needs at home, and some form of wake-up call is likely to come from our spouse or children. At work, we may focus on tasks and miss the relationship needs in the process. A wake-up call may come, for example, when employees stage a walkout.

Pause to examine the life issues shown in the Life Balance table and rank how well you are balancing each combination. Ranking the head-heart issues at a 3 suggests that these elements are in balance and working well in your life. If they lean toward 2 or 1, you will likely experience stress, dysfunction, and periodic wake-up calls!

Let's first examine the areas where you identified an effective balance, those ranked at 3:

- What are the benefits of being in balance?

- What specifically are you doing to achieve that balanced state?

105

- How do you feel about being in balance?

- What are the long-term results of being in balance?

Now explore the life issues that you perceive to be out of balance, those ranked 1 or 2:

- What is trying to happen in your life?

- What are the costs of not being in balance?

- What's the *worst* that could happen if you made a life adjustment?

- What's the *best* that could happen if you made a life adjustment?

- What if you decided to do nothing about the imbalance?

- What are you *willing* to do that would make a positive difference?

Balance, like health, is a natural state. Our bodies, inner being, and environment seek and reward balance. When it is not present, an unnatural state is reached that triggers internal signals to either make an adjustment or experience the consequences. Illness can often be our body's way of calling attention to the fact that we need to do something differently to return to a natural state of health. Organizations, like biological systems, may also become dysfunctional when they are out of balance.

You are in charge of your choices and behaviors. If an area of your life calls for attention, pause to make the head-heart connection. Listen and explore the many options that your internal board of directors might make available. Choice points await your attention. Experience the power of pausing.

Comfort, Stretch, and "Oops" Zones:
CHOOSING TO GROW

"Man's mind, once stretched by a new idea, never regains its original dimensions."

Oliver Wendell Holmes

We are seekers of comfort. Most of us do not want to be uncomfortable and therefore avoid physical and emotional conditions that contribute to our discomfort. Even homes and offices usually have thermostatically controlled environments that maintain a certain comfort zone. If it gets too hot, the air conditioner kicks in. If it gets too cold, the heater turns on. The thermostat, an automatic regulating mechanism, maintains the status quo within acceptable limits.

We human beings also have our own built-in automatic regulating mechanism. We establish our own behavioral comfort zones related to standards of performance and how we see ourselves. By defining our limits within the comfort zone, we simultaneously define who we are.

Within each of us is a part that wants to change and a part that doesn't. Even your decision to read this book suggests that a part of you is interested in changing, growing, and learning. Both parts, the part that wants to change and the part that doesn't, exist within us simultaneously. Sometimes this "I want to change–I don't want to change" message confuses us and others.

Think back, for example, to when you were about to get married. Part of you was ready to charge ahead, while another part of your being may have resisted the change. Consider also your first day on a new job. The "adventuresome" part of you was excited, but the "security" part found it difficult to be fully present. Which part usually "wins" for you—the adventuresome or the security part?

The Comfort Zone

When coasting in our comfort zones, we don't grow. We continue to do more of the same—the same thoughts, feelings, ideas, and behaviors. While this is certainly an appropriate strategy at times, maintaining the status quo limits our behavioral options. The narrower the zone, the fewer options there are. The wider the zone, the more options there are. This zone can be expanded, however, to include what we learn in both the stretch and "oops" zones.

Maintaining a comfort zone can, paradoxically, lead to discomfort in the long run. If by being comfortable we avoid important life issues, internal tension accumulates. We often sense, in our heart of hearts, the need for change in our career development, relationships, physical condition, financial security, or spiritual connection. Eventually, as both internal and external pressures for change persist, the "comfort zone" ceases to serve us.

On the other hand, the comfort zone can be a resource for rest and rejuvenation. While growth does not occur in

STRETCH ZONE
Your Growing Edge

COMFORT ZONE

"OOPS" ZONE
No Failure—Only Feedback

this state, the comfort zone provides a respite that enables us to reflect, enjoy ourselves, and position ourselves for future growth.

The Stretch Zone

A difference exists between where you are now and where you want to be. Extending into this new zone requires leaving your comfort zone and *stretching*. The stretch zone, also known as your *growing edge,* generates both fear and excitement.

Think of a stretch time in your life, either personally or professionally, when you accomplished something exceptionally well. You were hot, unstoppable! Reflect back on your self-talk. Chances are, you will hear such phrases as "I can conquer the world." "I am hot!" "I did it!" "Damn, I'm good!" "This feels good!" Listen to those reassuring voices.

109

For many of us, another set of voices surfaces in the stretch zone. These voices sound something like this: "That's not like me." "I'll never keep this up." "Now the pressure is on! I don't think I can do it." "Be realistic!" We go into resistance. Our internal air conditioner kicks in, cools us off, and pulls us back down into our comfort zone! Can you relate to those voices as well? We can't picture ourselves continuing to function in the stretch zone. We establish upper limits and make behavioral adjustments to bring us back down to the place that most closely matches the picture we have of ourselves—the comfort zone. This is called "the retreat to the familiar."

By being willing to be uncomfortable for a while, to experiment, to stick to it, and to make mistakes, we can make a difference in our lives and in those around us. By reaching into our stretch zones, we simultaneously expand our comfort zones to include this new level of functioning. Remember the time you made your first public speech? Clearly outside of your comfort zone, right? Yet by making speech after speech, you expanded your comfort zone to include this activity at a higher level of competence and confidence.

The "Oops" Zone

As we grow and develop, we make mistakes, and we end up in the "oops" zone. In this zone, there is no failure, only feedback. An IBM story clearly demonstrates this point. It seems that a young vice president made an error that cost IBM ten million dollars. Since the loss occurred when ten million dollars was considered to be a lot of money, Thomas Watson, Jr., then president of IBM, invited the young man into his office to discuss the situation. (Can you imagine yourself being invited into the president's office to explain a ten-million-dollar mistake? How would you like that one on your résumé?) The associate quietly said, "I suppose you want my resignation." Mr. Watson replied, "You must be kidding—we have ten million dollars invested in your education!" Imagine the commitment level of the young man toward IBM at that point. It probably took him all of four days to come up with ideas to earn that money back.

Recently, when I interviewed an IBM veteran of nine years, he explained, "We don't punish people for making mistakes. If we did, all that we would teach them is not to take risks. We can't afford that." There is no failure, only temporary setbacks. Some individuals attempt to find culprits and nail them to the wall. Taken to an extreme, finding flaws encourages others to take lower risks and channel their creativity to focus on covering themselves rather than enhancing their performance.

There is no failure, only feedback. Thomas Edison would never have succeeded in creating the light bulb if he had been sidetracked by the thousands of "failures" he experienced in its development. Instead, each experiment provided important feedback that drew him closer to a successful result. Colonel Harland Sanders, at a ripe old age, experienced over one thousand rejections for his now famous chicken recipe. The cleaning product Formula 409—you've got it—had 408 "unsuccessful" attempts before the final product was developed. Clearly, successful people have more "failures" than failures do.

> *"If you want to increase your success rate, double your failure rate."*
>
> Thomas Watson, Sr., founder of IBM

Provide a safe environment in which you and others can make mistakes. Convert these experiences into learning opportunities. Instead of asking, "Why does this always happen to me?" ask, "What can I learn from this?" Key into the wake-up call and discover how the "oops" zone can be transformed into still another positive learning experience.

Learning opportunities abound outside our comfort zone. Our personal and professional value increases when we stretch beyond the safety of our comfort zone. Stretch and "oops" zones are friends in disguise. Those who choose to tap into these resources experience new dimensions of growth. Although **111** stretching involves risk, greater long-term peril often results from staying within the comfort zone.

AWARENESS CHECKS

◗ Where are you choosing comfort over growth?

◗ How can you move your life forward by choosing to venture more deeply into the stretch zone?

◗ What is the learning now?

Wake-up calls. Choice points.

"The best way to make your dreams come true is to wake up."

Paul Valéry

Low Risk Equals High Risk:

RISKING FOR GREATER GAINS

"Avoiding danger is no safer in
the long run than outright
exposure. Life is either a daring
adventure, or nothing."

Helen Keller

Risk involves taking action when the outcomes are unknown. What comes to mind when you think of taking risks? Threat? Fear? Challenge? Opportunity? To create new possibilities requires us to move outside our comfort zones and take risks that are intended to result in some form of gain. The potential cost, loss, or discomfort

113

associated with taking risks prevents many of us from moving off our position. Sometimes, however, the cost, loss, or discomfort of *not* taking risks can be even greater than the risks themselves.

"Shovel while the piles are small."

Author unknown

We seek comfort and safety. We dodge risks in an effort to avoid discomfort. Yet avoidance of short-term discomfort can result in greater long-term pain. We are likely to experience a wake-up call in those areas of our life in which we hold back or avoid accountability. Let's explore the life learning.

SOME YEARS AGO, A FRUSTRATED and angry department head came into my office seeking approval to immediately fire one of his employees who was performing poorly. The employee had worked in his department for over five years and had never been particularly effective. In fact, according to the department head, serious mistakes periodically interrupted the employee's mediocre performance. Two such blunders in the last week had prompted the department head to finally take action.

When he was asked what the employee knew about his chronic poor performance, the manager responded, "He has to know! He's been here for five years." Not finding that to be a satisfactory answer, I asked to see the employee's performance evaluations for the last five years. Sitting on the same side of the table, the manager and I placed the five evaluations in order and reviewed the findings. Each evaluation had overall ratings ranging from "satisfactory" to "outstanding." "I don't understand how these evaluations can be as good as they are when you say his performance has been so poor all this time." After a long pause, the department head quietly responded: "Well, I didn't want to hurt his feelings." We both learned from this experience.

114

The manager chose to take the low risk (and maintain his comfort zone) by not confronting and working through the performance issues early in the employee's career. By withholding the truth from the employee, he allowed performance problems to grow to an unmanageable stage. An initial low-risk approach evolved into a high-risk situation. Are you, personally or professionally, sitting on some important issue that requires attention?

"Shovel while the piles are small" becomes an important relationship practice at work and at home. Sometimes we let piles accumulate to the point where issues become too big to handle. When the piles are small, we tend to avoid the issues because of discomfort. When they are big, we avoid them because of the trauma and major work involved. By not dealing with the issues, we allow "stuff" to accumulate that drains energy and damages relationships.

"The chief danger in life is that you may take too many precautions."

Alfred Adler

The opposite of "low risk equals high risk" is *"high risk equals low risk."* By "risking" initially, we can often create a lower-risk result in the long run. Healthy relationships require clear, open, honest communication. While sharing what we feel, want, and think may appear to be risky, we are more likely to create lasting, quality relationships. By committing to shovel while the piles are small—telling our truth in a caring way—we allow internal and external relationships to prosper.

AFTER I EXPLORED THIS CONCEPT in one of my leadership development seminars, Jan, a participant, approached me during a break. "I don't buy that concept at all!" she exclaimed. "I did

115

exactly what you said in my first marriage for twenty years, and it didn't work. I trusted my husband at a high level, and he went out and had an affair. Our marriage went away. So much for your 'high risk equals low risk' theory!"

Standing in front of me was an angry, hurt, and confused woman. She *had* trusted at a high level and had been burned. She did exactly as I had proposed and paid a very large price. In her mind, therefore, the concept didn't work. In fact, no human dynamics formula works consistently. Clearly, some practices work better than others, and none are guaranteed.

I explored with Jan how that event had affected her life, particularly in her relationships with men. Jan had a one-word response to describe her interactions with men: "superficial." In fact, she had had six superficial relationships in a row with men since her divorce. Clearly, according to Jan, "Men cannot be trusted." "What do you want in your relationship with a man?" I asked. After thinking for a moment, she responded: "A deep, loving relationship with a foundation of mutual trust." I asked her, "On a scale of 0 to 10, to what extent do you trust men?" "Two!" she quickly responded.

Let's explore this further. When you give a 2 level of trust, what can you expect to get back in terms of trust? A 2 *or less.* Why would you get back less than you give? People tend to either trust or protect. The more you protect yourself from being vulnerable, open, and real, the less you trust. Sensing that you are holding back, others choose to hold back as well. The result? Mutual trust declines as each person waits to determine whether the other is safe. Lack of trust tends to produce a self-fulfilling response.

So how do you go about building a foundation of trust—especially when you were "burned" for trusting at a high level? At what level are you willing to trust after you have been violated? Low? Medium? High? What are the costs and benefits of each level? What relationship results may be experienced?

How do you get out of the low-trust cycle? Some suggest playing it safe and trusting at a low level. By seeing how the other person behaves, you can determine your own course of action.

Of course, the other person matches your withholding behavior and both of you remain stuck! Jan created a repetitive pattern of low-level trusting and consistently attracted jerks into her life. What she received reflected what she was willing to give. No wonder a gap in trust develops. No wonder people have such a difficult time connecting.

Others suggest trusting at a middle level, not too high and not too low. In this way, relationship safety can be checked out without getting burned too badly if someone takes advantage of our "trusting" position. We determine our response by placing the burden on the other person to demonstrate trustworthiness first. This approach, however, clearly gives our relationship-building power over to the other person.

"When we hold back on life, life holds back on us."

Mary Manin Boggs

I had a personal experience with this concept when I was being counseled at the close of my marriage. I tend to trust people at a high level, and the marriage counselor said to me, "Eric, you are crazy for trusting people at such a high level. Instead, trust at a 5. If they trust you more, you have a bonus. If they trust you less, you haven't lost very much."

When a psychologist says you are crazy, it's time to sit up and take note! Perhaps I should listen to this guy! Because of my trusting nature, his advice went to the very core of my philosophy. For several months I reflected on his words—and finally rejected his council.

When you trust at level 5, what are you likely to get back? A 5 or less. I don't want 5s in my interactions with others—I want much more. If I want an 8, 9, or even 10 coming back, I had better be prepared to give what I expect. Life experience teaches that we generally get back what we put out. If we don't like what we are getting back, we should examine what we are putting out. **117**

Yes, others have taken advantage of me for trusting at a high level. Some individuals have used me because I trusted them, just as the psychologist said. And I can count the times that happened in my entire life on one hand. Conversely, the advantages of trusting at a high level have been so great, both for me and for others, that I cannot even begin to count the positive experiences. When I compare the lifetime costs versus the benefits of trusting, I find it easy to trust at a high level.

I am not suggesting that we take unreasonable or unsafe risks. I wouldn't park my unlocked car, full of valuables, in a high-crime district. I wouldn't loan money to an escaped felon and expect to be paid back. I am suggesting, however, that we consciously expand our interpersonal risk taking to experience more peace of mind, joy, and connectedness. Low risk equals high risk and high risk equals low risk.

How are you likely to respond if someone trusts you at a very high level? Most people reciprocate with a high level of trust. Conversely, if they are distrusted, people tend to fulfill those expectations as well. This is called the *law of reciprocity*. Here is an example.

A NEW CLIENT INVITED ME TO WORK with them to improve communication, trust, and overall morale. This large corporation had a history of labor strife, grievance, and patterns of "we-they" behavior. When I initially worked with this new client, I conducted numerous interviews and reviewed the company's human resource policies. The manual for new employees was particularly revealing. On page 1 of a rather thick, legalistic document, eight reasons were listed for terminating an employee from the organization! The manual began with a full-page "advertisement" listing reasons for being fired! No welcome to the organization, no empowering or encouraging statements. Instead, an introduction that read like a declaration of war between management and labor.

As a new employee, how would you feel if you were handed a book of regulations that clearly said that you could not be trusted? How would you behave in those circumstances? Which behaviors would be stimulated: your best or your worst? This organization's behavior compares with Jan's individual behavior in that both wanted to develop high levels of trust but were unwilling to give it.

"If you don't invest very much, then defeat doesn't hurt very much and winning is not very exciting."

Dick Vermeil, NFL coach

Let's explore trust in relationships even further. If we are not sure of a relationship, holding back or taking a low risk becomes our typical response. When the relationship does not work out, we might say to ourselves, "It's a good thing I held back. I could have used up all my good stuff on this person and not had anything left for the next special person to arrive in my life!" We will never know, however, if the relationship failed because we held back or because it was not a good fit.

Now for the stretch. If you are not sure of a relationship, I encourage you to give 100 percent. Be in the relationship fully. Give your fullest—unconditionally. Chances are, the relationship will work. If it doesn't work, then you will know that it is because the relationship itself is not a good fit rather than because of a lack of commitment on your part. High risk equals low risk.

You might be asking, "Why should I take all the risks? What about the other person?" You are in charge of your feelings, beliefs, and actions. And you teach others how to behave toward you. While you cannot change other people, you can influence them through your own behaviors and actions. By being a living role model of what you want to receive from others, you create more of what you want in your life.

119

*"Progress always involves risk;
you can't steal second base
and keep your foot on first."*

Frederick Wilcox

The president of one of my client companies said to his management team, "I want you to take risks, and you better not make any mistakes!" What did he teach his associates? Giving mixed messages like this communicates a lack of safety and support for taking risks. People then generally choose to stay in their comfort zone—to play it safe. In the long run, both the individuals and the organization have begun a journey toward obsolescence. If only the risks that pay off are rewarded, we are teaching people not to take risks. And our competitors gain the edge!

Another client has an annual Risk Takers' Dinner, which honors individuals whose prudent risk taking paid off— and those whose didn't! In this organization, employees are encouraged and rewarded for their innovative spirit and willingness to stretch outside their comfort zone. Both the employees and the organization win through a proliferation of new ideas that positions the company to provide superior products and services. In this environment, by contrast, people feel it is safe to take risks.

Risks fall into a variety of categories—physical, interpersonal, career, financial, social, and even spiritual. One person might be comfortable taking physical risks, yet find sharing feelings terribly unnerving. Another might share feelings easily, yet become immobilized at the thought of speaking in public. We all have our stretches. We all hold back in some areas of our life, but in the areas we resist are often our greatest opportunities to learn and grow. In the spirit of personal growth, I encourage you to experiment with some form of risk taking that will make a positive difference in your life without being harmful to yourself or others. How might you profit by taking risks in the following areas?

- Spouse or partner risks (sharing what you want, feel, or think)

- Friendship risks (sharing feelings, dealing with unresolved conflict)

- Work or career risks (seeking a promotion, changing jobs)

- Financial risks (setting up a significant retirement program, investing)

- Educational risks (taking classes outside your field, getting a degree)

- Physical risks (climbing a mountain, participating in team sports)

- Spiritual risks (making a spiritual commitment, attending a retreat)

- Material risks (purchasing a car or house, letting go of "excesses")

- Emotional risks (dealing with unresolved issues, looking inward)

AWARENESS CHECKS

In which of the above categories do you experience the most comfort in risk taking? The most resistance?

What is the learning?

Creating new possibilities requires you to move outside of your comfort zone. New life dimensions await you beyond that wall of resistance. Low risk equals high risk and high risk equals low risk.   **121**

Completing Your Incompletes:
NEW BEGINNINGS

"Now is the time."

Martin Luther King

Unfinished business. Incompletes. Energy drainers. We all have parts of our life that require attention, yet we sometimes talk ourselves out of doing what we know needs to be done. And our inaction frequently consumes more energy than would be required to deal with the actual issue! Let's explore the relationship between what happens "out there" and your internal experience.

Your body has subtle and not-so-subtle ways of directing you to issues that require attention. Like a highly sensitive biofeedback instrument, your body provides important and often immediate information to which you should pay attention. For example, where in your body do you feel stress? It might be your shoulders, your lower back, or your jaw, or it might take the form of a headache. Imagine that you are about to withhold important information from someone. Where do you feel it? In your chest, or perhaps your shoulders? What if you tell a significant lie? Do you feel it in your throat or jaw? If you are tossing and turning between 2:00 and 4:00 A.M. rather than having a restful sleep, your body may be sending the message "Wake up! Wake up! You have unfinished business requiring attention."

Pay attention to your internal "body talk." Your body does not lie. By working in close connection with your internal body signals, you can teach yourself to pause when you first receive "notice" of unfinished business. When you receive an inner signal, look for the learning.

AWARENESS CHECKS

- What message is my body trying to tell me right now?

- What am I avoiding?

- Am I on automatic pilot rather than being awake and aware?

- Am I going in a direction that may not be a good fit?

- What should I let go of that I no longer need to carry?

- What can I do right now that will make a positive difference?

- What is the learning right now?

Remarkable growth advances, both personal and professional, occur when we pay attention to and act on inner body messages. Not some mystic process practiced only by spiritual gurus in mountain caves, intuitive qualities have pragmatic applications today at work and at home. A few centuries ago, intuitive individuals were thought to be witches and were burned at the stake. Now that same intuitive quality is a fundamental requirement of effective corporate leaders. The Fortune 500 companies, more often than not, recruit presidents who have both sound business savvy and the ability to assess and act upon intangible, intuitive leadership elements. In my work with peak-performing leaders, I have found that they regularly enhance the quality of their judgment and decisions by listening to their internal resources.

Break the pattern of your incompletes.

Let us apply the concept of our inner body's message to an important element of life—*incompletes*. An incomplete is anything that drains internal energy when you think of it. This inner body signal communicates the message that unfinished business awaits your attention. Your body brings a choice point into your awareness. You can either react and recycle history or respond—and do something differently to bring about better results. Conscious responding creates an opportunity for new beginnings.

In addition to draining energy, incompletes detract from our ability to experience fulfillment in other areas of our life. They also function as a barrier to expressing full creativity and often prevent us from moving forward when we "numb out." The cost of incompletes can be great.

Perhaps a brief journey might assist in identifying where you experience incompletes. Bring to mind an individual with whom you have unfinished business (unresolved conflicts, withheld forgiveness, unspoken appreciation). Picture this person clearly and experience the energy drain as you focus on the incomplete. How many years has this incomplete gone unattended and unfinished? What payoffs and costs are you experiencing by allowing it to go unattended?

125

Some people with whom I have worked experience incompletes with others that date back decades. Their behavioral patterns recycle the same old stuff, without ever making progress. The resulting stuck state consumes enormous internal energy. Like water in a leaking faucet, the lost resources could eventually fill a pond. And these may be only a few of many incompletes they are avoiding.

Continuing on your journey, imagine returning home from work and driving into your garage. The car barely fits into a space limited by boxes, old discards, and various forms of junk that you are "going to take care of sometime." Another incomplete.

Walking into the living room, you pass by a green-and-blue Mediterranean-style couch. While it was once considered stylish, the couch now ranks among the world's ugliest! Just being in its presence drains your energy. For years, you have hated that couch, yet you continue to keep it in your life. Another incomplete.

You now go to the bedroom to change into something more comfortable. Opening the closet doors, you observe a large section consisting of clothes that have not been worn for more than a year. You have hung on to them because you thought that they would come back into style someday. Actually, you would not be caught dead wearing those rags, but they continue to occupy space in your closet and deplete energy from your being.

Examine your personal and professional life. Where might incompletions be draining your positive energy? Some of us have multiple sources of energy drainers. The following categories might be of assistance in identifying your incompletes. You may have relationship incompletes with your spouse, children, parents, boss, friends, co-workers, next door neighbor, former spouse, and former spouse's attorney, among others.

Relationship incompletes:

- Having unresolved conflict

- Not showing appreciation

- Withholding forgiveness

- Having important unexpressed feelings

How can you break the pattern of the incompletes that have demanded so much of your energy and attention and move on? If you are serious about doing something differently, prepare yourself for both self-examination and taking action. Two dimensions are important to consider: your incompletes and your resources. Draw a line down the center of a sheet of paper, labeling the left column "My Incompletes" and the other "My Resources." Become quiet inside, reflect on your unfinished business, and list all the issues that drain your energy. Notice the patterns of your incompletes. Are they more relationship- or task-oriented? What do you resist most? What learning do you experience about the nature and content of your incompletes?

Making a Positive Difference

My Incompletes: *My Resources:*

_____   _____

_____   _____

_____   _____

_____   _____

_____   _____

_____   _____

_____   _____

Step 1: List all your *incompletes*—anything that drains energy. Include relationship, integrity, career, financial, physical, material, personal, and spiritual issues.

Step 2: List any internal and external *resources* that could potentially assist in addressing these issues. Include personal talents (at least five), friends, family, and spiritual resources that could make a positive contribution.

Step 3: Identify your three most significant incompletes with a star. (Note possible patterns. Are they more relationship- or task-related?)

Step 4: Identify any and all resources with a star that could assist in completing your significant incompletes.

Step 5: Explore specific steps you would be willing to take today to make a positive difference. Commit to action!

129

Now list both the *internal* and *external* resources that are available to you. Pay particular attention to your own talents, skills, and abilities. This is not a time to be modest: List no fewer than five of your strengths. Also list such external resources as specific people and financial, material, and spiritual resources.

Again becoming quiet inside, identify your three most significant incompletes, putting a star by each one in the margin of the page. Experience the cost and pain of not dealing with these issues. Notice that this is familiar territory, since these feelings have been recirculated for some time.

Now refer to your list of resources and place a star in the margin beside each one that could make a positive contribution to the completion of your incompletes. If you feel that your resources are not enough to work through the incompletes, seek out additional external resources such as a counselor to assist with the process. While most answers are within you, securing external counsel is prudent when appropriate.

With your significant incompletes in mind, explore the following questions:

AWARENESS CHECKS

- What do I want–what are my interests?
- What do other people want—what are their interests?
- What is the *worst* that could happen if I addressed this incomplete?
  - Can I handle the worst? If not, what additional external resources do I need?
  - If I can handle the worst, then I can proceed.
- What is the *best* that could happen if I addressed this incomplete?
- What if I did *not* address this incomplete?
- What specific action can I take today that will make a positive difference?

Use this time for a quiet pause, and listen as your "internal board of directors" guides you through the choice points. By reflecting on these six awareness checks, you will obtain greater insight about converting your incompletes into completes. In particular, compare the third question with the fifth. Which has the greater long-term cost: addressing or avoiding the issue? Of the literally thousands of people with whom I have worked, the vast majority find the cost of avoiding an issue to be greater than the cost of addressing it.

"Only you yourself can be your liberator."
Wilhelm Reich

WHEN I WAS FIRST INTRODUCED TO THE CON-CEPT of incompletes in a personal growth seminar years ago, I listed mine. The list was lengthy; many issues drained energy from my life at that time. In fact, this process became an important wake-up call.

Forgiveness, a significant incomplete on my list, boldly stood out. Two people required forgiveness: "Darrell" and "Eric." Darrell, a good friend, minister, and marriage counselor, became an issue. Let me explain. When my former wife and I reached our most difficult relationship choice point, I frequently talked with Darrell by long-distance telephone. He was helpful, caring, and supportive.

My wife also began talking on the telephone to Darrell. She also found him to be helpful, caring, and supportive. They began to talk more frequently, and soon a relationship formed between them. She ultimately flew off to meet him for an extended weekend. I felt violated and used. One of my best friends and my wife together—I thought this only happened to other people! She and I had just separated. Until then, I had resisted a divorce. Their rendezvous pushed me over the edge.

I generally do not harbor much anger in my life and am considered to be a relatively calm person. Yet this event acti- **131** vated my hot buttons. When my wife returned, I called Darrell and "talked" with him about the situation. "Screamed" might be a better description! After using up every swear word I knew in my one-sided conversation, I invented new ones! Never before had I experienced such a "colorful" exchange with anyone, let alone with a friend.

When I was through, I slammed the receiver down and said to myself, "There, that takes care of Darrell." I had just participated in a long-distance form of revenge with a friend. Little did I know, however, what the result would be for me. Even though I felt violated and used by Darrell, what I did to *him* in that telephone conversation did not feel good at all. He was a friend, and I had violated *him*. I had created a new incomplete. Even though my behavior might have been justified to others, how I treated him generated troublesome feelings within myself.

For two years, every time I thought of Darrell, energy left my body. My inner body signals were clear, yet I did not know how to read them at the time. I did not know how to pause, become quiet inside, and look for the learning. I continued to sleepwalk through my wake-up calls and to focus on the "injustice" that Darrell and my former wife had perpetrated on me. In my effort to assume the victim position, I missed the learning. I missed why she felt a need to go somewhere else to develop a relationship. I missed how I contributed to the decline of our relationship. I consumed energy looking "out there" when I could have benefited by looking inward.

When I addressed my incompletes in the personal growth seminar, I discovered that "Darrell" and "Eric" both required forgiveness. When reflecting on both situations, I asked:

- What message is my body trying to tell me right now?

- What is the learning?

- What am I avoiding?

- What consequences will I experience by following this direction?

- What can I do right now that will make a positive difference?

With Darrell, time had been a great healer, and I began to understand that he had nothing to do with the demise of my first marriage. Instead, he was symptomatic of a much larger relationship issue. If it had not been Darrell, someone else would have been the catalyst. I could finally bring myself to forgive him for the "violation" I experienced and I drew a line through his name, symbolizing that forgiveness.

Yet *my* name still remained on the list. Why did I find it difficult to draw a line through my own name? Why was I unable to strike it from the list of incompletes? I began listening to my inner body signals. What is the message? What am I avoiding? Could her departure have something to do with *me?*

Even though I had reached the stage of forgiving Darrell and forgiving myself for the way I treated him, I continued to experience an energy drain—not as much of a drain, but a drain nevertheless. I got even quieter and the learning became clear. I needed to *talk* with Darrell. I needed to forgive him and be forgiven. Then I would be able to convert the incomplete into a complete.

I had not talked with Darrell for nearly 2½ years, but I placed the long-distance call. After a number of rings, his answering machine engaged. The recorded message said, "Hi! This is Darrell. I am in search of love, truth, and joy. After finding these, I will return your call!" His message threw me. At the sound of the beep, I said, "Darrell, this is Eric. I would like to talk with you in a very different way than I did a few years ago. Please give me a call."

About six weeks later, late one evening, my telephone rang. In a soft-spoken voice, Darrell identified himself. We talked. We really communicated. We even cried. We forgave and were forgiven. Each of us converted an incomplete into a complete.

While our friendship did not survive this traumatic life event, peace of mind has been restored, certainly for me and, I am confident, for Darrell as well. Whenever I think of him, I experience completion and literally no energy drain. What a difference! Instead of siphoning off my creativity, blaming others, and emotionally poisoning myself with negative thoughts, I experienced internal harmony. I began a new stage of growth in my life journey.

133

The way out is through.

After tending to an incomplete, a test of successful conversion is to ask yourself: "When I think of the situation, do I continue to experience a drain of energy?" If your inner body response is *yes,* then continue looking for the learning. If it is *no,* then celebrate your completion! Honor yourself for having had the courage to face and work through your incompletions. When you address an issue, peace of mind ultimately follows.

Not all incompletes have solutions. Letting go and moving on can be the wisest decision when conditions or circumstances cannot be changed. Just accepting "what is" can be the most prudent course of action. An important coping strategy involves learning to peacefully accept what we cannot control. The Alcoholics Anonymous Serenity Prayer says it well:

> God, grant me the serenity to accept the things I cannot change, the courage to change the things I can, and the wisdom to know the difference.

What stands between you and your higher good? What detracts from your wholeness? What blocks you from a new beginning? Turning incompletions into completions requires awareness and courage. Yet even the process of clearing up incompletions energizes and empowers you to experience life at a more fulfilling level. You can progress from a numb state to an alive state. Awareness of an incompletion is a wake-up call. Choose to make a positive difference, first, by not collecting new incompletions, and second, by promptly addressing existing completions in a way that honors yourself and others. Moving from unfinished business to completions lightens your journey and enables you to experience inner joy. The way out is through.

Part 3

TALKING
STRAIGHT

13

Tuning In:
THE MESSAGE
BEHIND THE MESSAGE

"You cannot _not_ communicate."

Richard Bandler and John Grinder

"I'VE NEVER LIKED OUR VACATIONS!" said my first wife while we were on holiday in our twelfth year of marriage. The significance of this indirect message sailed right over my head. As I described in Chapter 1, my snooze alarm was engaged and I missed the wake-up call. In retrospect, many lessons were eventually to be learned as a result of this statement. But then, instead of pausing, listening, and seeking understanding, I became defensive. I said things like, "But you've helped plan our vacations! We've gone here and we've gone there. I can't believe you waited all these years to tell me this!"

Listen for both the message—and the message behind the message.

WHEN THEY COMMUNICATE, PEOPLE SOMETIMES have a message (the spoken words) and a message behind the message (their real feelings, thoughts, and wants). I thought my wife was talking about our *vacations*. Wrong! She was talking about our *relationship!* She didn't want to be on vacation with *me!* My "awareness" consisted primarily of deletions and distortions of reality. The result? I missed the very essence of her indirect message. (Remember—what you focus on determines what you miss.)

In our fifteenth year of marriage (we were still hanging in there!), I came home only to learn that she was going on vacation—with one of my best buddies! I said, "But you don't even *like* vacations!" I still didn't get it. I continued to focus on the message and missed the far more important message behind the message.

For two years, I blamed her for our divorce. It had come completely out of the blue. She never *told* me about her real thoughts. In fact, I was planning a major fifteenth-year anniversary celebration while she was planning our separation! Talk about being out of touch! For fifteen years, I was sleepwalking through our marriage. When the inevitable wake-up call finally penetrated, she was gone! A major surprise!

In truth, her departure was no surprise. She "told" me, in only about a thousand ways, of her dissatisfaction with our relationship. Yes, the messages were indirect. Yet if I had been willing (or perhaps able) to listen with a head-heart connection, I would have received the messages. Sleepwalking is a costly way to approach both relationships and life. You snooze, you loose!

A number of years ago, researchers at Stanford University reached a startling conclusion related to interpersonal communication. In a carefully controlled study, they found that only 7 percent of communication results from actual spoken words— *what* is being said. Ninety-three percent of our inner state is expressed through tone, tempo, pitch, volume, and body physi-ology—*how* we communicate. Reading nonverbal signals is, therefore, an essential part of effective communication at work and home.

What happens on the outside tends to mirror our internal experience.

You don't really know what is going on inside of others. All you get is their BMIRs—behaviorally mani-fested internal responses. BMIRs provide external clues about another person's internal experience. They are usually expressed or disclosed in three forms: visual, auditory, and kinesthetic. Drawing on your own experience, what observations can you make about the following forms of nonverbal communication? Notice how these signals may communicate even more than words themselves.

Visual BMIRs (what you see):
Glazed eyes versus bright eyes
Frown versus smile
Folded arms versus open body
Shallow chest breathing versus deep belly breathing
Pale versus flushed skin
Large versus small pupils
Direct versus fixed or shifting eye contact

Auditory BMIRs (what you hear):
Slow talk versus fast talk
Low pitch versus high pitch
Soft talk versus loud talk
Direct conversation versus indirect conversation

139

Formal speech versus informal speech

Flowing conversation versus selected words

Kinesthetic BMIRs (what you feel):

Cool, moist hands versus warm, dry hands

Stiff hug versus soft hug

Distance versus closeness

Safe versus guarded posture

Richard Bandler and John Grinder, in their work on neurolinguistic programming, concluded, "You cannot *not* communicate." You are always communicating and influencing others, primarily through your BMIRs and secondarily through your words. Your choice is *how* you want to communicate and what results you are seeking.

Paying attention to the full communication process, including both words and BMIRs, has significant implications at work and home. Rather than coming to conclusions about the meaning of BMIRs, observe their signals to enhance your interpersonal understanding.

To build our understanding and enhance relationships, we must learn to decode BMIRs. Becoming aware that they exist is the first step. By consciously being present when we interact with others, we can train ourselves to increase our awareness of their state of being by monitoring their changing BMIRs. Instead of interpreting these signals and possibly coming to erroneous conclusions, we decode BMIRs through direct, nonjudgmental interaction with other people. Let's apply this concept:

BMIR Observation.   When you come home from work, your spouse gives you an unusually long and clingy hug (kinesthetic BMIR), looks down at the floor (visual BMIR), and speaks in a softer tone with a slower pace (auditory BMIR); however, she makes no mention of any situation that might have influenced her day.

BMIR Decoding. Rather than concluding that she is having an affair, pause and give nonjudgmental, sensory-specific feedback: "I noticed that you are talking in a softer voice and gave me a longer hug than usual. I'm available to listen if you want to talk." At that point, tears flow as she shares the results of her laboratory tests from the doctor's office.

BMIR Observation. When you delegate a new, challenging project to one of your peak-performing employees, you anticipate that she will be excited and rise to the opportunity. Instead, her face reddens (kinesthetic BMIR displayed visually), she speaks with hesitation (auditory BMIR), and she looks away while slumping in her chair (visual BMIR).

BMIR Decoding. You might conclude that she either doesn't like the assignment or is overloaded with other work. This is a time for nonjudgmental, sensory-specific feedback! "I thought you would be excited about this project, but I noticed that you looked away, spoke with hesitation, and settled into your chair. I'm open to exploring your feelings and interests." At that point, the employee feels safe enough to share the fact that she just received an unsolicited job offer that represents an important career jump. Now that she is faced with choosing between two jobs she enjoys, she is confused.

Talking does not necessarily mean that you are communicating.

Just because you are talking does not mean that you are communicating. When your words say one thing and your BMIRs infer another, the resulting mixed messages are likely to be misinterpreted or viewed with suspicion. Mixed messages undermine trust and encourage others to make assumptions about what we are thinking, feeling, and wanting. A *negative* intent is more likely to be assumed in the absence of direct feedback as people look for some hidden agenda or message behind the message. Effective communication matches our outer expression (what we say) with our internal experience (what we are thinking, feeling, and wanting).

A PROFESSIONAL COUPLE CAR-POOLED HOME from work one evening. The husband, one of these pedal-to-the-metal drivers, pressed heavily on the accelerator as he maneuvered through traffic. As telephone poles and signs whizzed by, his wife said, "Oh look! They're having a grand opening at that new restaurant." Hubby responded, "Yup." A little while later, she noticed another restaurant sign advertising a "seafood spectacular" and called it to his attention. Same response. Shortly thereafter, he drove into their garage, picked up the newspaper, then settled into an easy chair to read the sports section.

While he was quietly reading, he became aware of noises in the kitchen—cupboard doors slamming, dishes banging on the counter. Now, this guy was no fool. His sensors said, "Alert! Alert! Something is amiss!" He cautiously walked into the kitchen and found his wife preparing dinner. "What's wrong?" he asked. "Nothing!" responded his wife with that all-too-familiar sound in her voice that signals trouble. Hubby then said, "Come on, now, something is bothering you." "I didn't want to fix dinner. I wanted to go out," she finally affirmed. With a confused look on his face, he asked, "Why didn't you tell me?" "I did—twice," she stated with certainty. He looked even more confused. Another message behind the message.

Sometimes adults are so indirect, tactful, diplomatic, and "sophisticated" in their communication that others do not have the slightest idea what they are talking about! Young children, on the other hand, are completely clear in their communication. It's easy to tell what a three-year-old wants, thinks, and feels. He or she tells you directly! And his or her words and BMIRs match. Children have not yet learned to be indirect or to hide their real feelings, thoughts, and wants. They simply share their inner states as if that's what they are supposed to do! Insecurity and inhibitions are not a part of the early childhood communication experience. Notice how *easy* it is to communicate with a child.

SOME YEARS AGO, WE INVITED A FAMILY to our home for a gourmet dinner. Sitting on several telephone books in a chair, their three-year-old joined us at the dinner table. When the gourmet delight was placed in front of him, his response was what you might expect from a little boy: "Yuk!" Horrified at these poor manners, his mother promptly scolded: "That's not nice! Now you tell them that you like the dinner." With hesitation in his voice, he said, "I like it." The process of learning to be less than honest had started. Children must be terribly confused by adults who tell them not to lie, yet teach them how to hide their real feelings; how to convey something other than their true inner state through manners, tact, and diplomacy; and how to play relationship games.

Interpersonal communication is not nearly as complex as we make it out to be. It's just a matter of exchanging our thoughts, feelings, and desires in an open and caring way. Yet we are often taught more about how to suppress these important inner states than to express them. Our communication would be vastly enhanced by combining the skills of an adult with the ability of a child to speak directly. Match your external words with your internal experience. Clarity of communication frees your spirit while building healthy relationships. And when you talk straight, fewer wake-up calls will have to blast their way through your protective barriers.

"Between whom there is hearty truth, there is hearty love."

Henry David Thoreau

143

The Simplicity of Truth:
TELLING IT STRAIGHT

"Truth is the grand simplifier."

Will Schutz

What if we chose to tell the truth, as we know it, at home and at work for the next six months? (Talk about wake-up calls!) What a scary proposition! Alarms go off with just the thought of revealing our real selves to others. What would they think? What would happen within our primary relationship? How would our boss respond? What consequences, both positive and negative, might we experience?

Truth is simply "what is." Awareness is the truth about myself I am willing to let pass through my many protective barriers. While "*my* truth" as I experience it may differ from "*the* truth," understanding occurs in an environment that supports an exchange of mutual truths. To communicate my truth to you, according to Will Schutz (1979), I "must be both aware and honest." Communicating with integrity—telling the truth—has been espoused by every major religious master for thousands of years. Yet sharing our truth remains a difficult communication choice for many of us.

Awareness and honesty are truly fundamental to building quality relationships. Caring straight talk increases mutual awareness, encourages growth, and provides a foundation for quality relationships. The amount of truth each of us is willing to share with others becomes a baseline for the intimacy of our relationship.

> ### *"If you tell the truth,*
> ### *you don't have to remember anything."*
>
> Mark Twain

Intellectually, most people buy into the value of telling the truth. Yet from a practical perspective, behaviors often do not support this concept. We avoid telling the truth out of fear of hurting others, fear of being uncomfortable, or fear of anticipated consequences. As a result, we choose to share something that is contrary to our awareness (active lying) or to withhold something about which we are aware (passive lying). Both choices deenergize us while creating tension in our relationships.

We become so diplomatic, indirect, tactful, and sophisticated in our communication that others do not have the slightest idea what we are talking about! Comedian Swami Beyondananda refers to these conditions as "truth decay"! When we do not share our thoughts, wants, and feelings directly, others have to guess about them. The relationship costs of this type of passive communication can be great. Caring straight talk, on the other hand, clarifies, simplifies, and facilitates the development of positive, committed relationships. How we communicate, therefore, is an important life choice point.

I have explored the advantages and disadvantages of telling the truth with thousands of people in professional development seminars. Their responses might be of interest:

Perceptions of Truth

Disadvantages of Truth:	*Advantages of Truth:*
It may hurt others.	It builds relationships.
It's risky.	It simplifies communication.
It's uncomfortable.	It builds respect.
It may cause relationship loss.	I don't have to "remember" what I said.
It may increase stress.	It releases stress.
It may increase conflict.	It builds trust.
It may make me vulnerable.	It usually resolves issues.
It's awkward.	It energizes.
It consumes energy.	It builds long-term credibility.
I might get the truth back!	It forces choice points.
It forces choice points.	It facilitates getting what I want.
I might be wrong.	It gives me peace of mind.
	It increases awareness.
	It encourages healing.
	It requires fewer trips to the confessional.

In examining these responses, it would appear that telling the truth is dependent upon circumstances. Many people conclude that, while they themselves want to be told the truth, others do not want to hear it! Go inside yourself and ask, "Do I **147** want to be told the truth at home and at work?" "What are the costs and benefits of being told the truth?" "What are the costs and benefits of not being told the truth?"

> ## *"If you do not tell the truth about yourself, you cannot tell it about other people."*
>
> Virginia Woolf

Gary Koyen, an important teacher to me at a transitional period in my life, introduced the concept of "real me" and "facade" communication. Learning continues as I apply this concept to communication at home and in my professional environments. Expanding on Koyen's concepts, I will explore four straight-talk communication conditions:

1. "Real Me"-to-Facade Transition

2. Facade-to-Facade Communication

3. "Real Me"-to-"Real Me" Communication

4. "Real Me"-to-Facade Communication

Condition 1: "Real Me"-to-Facade Transition

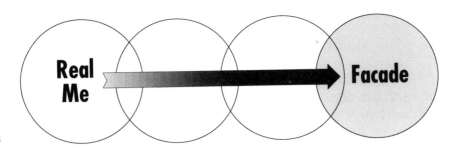

In Condition 1, the "Real Me" represents who I am—what I think, feel, value, and want. The Real Me can often best be captured in observing the behaviors of young children. You always know what they are feeling and wanting—they tell you in so many ways! Communicating with a young child can be so refreshing. No guesswork, no political games, no hidden agendas. Their Real Me behaviors match their inner experience.

Beginning early in life, however, we are conditioned not to be honest with our inner experience. We are sometimes taught to hide, withhold, modify, or suppress our inner beings to the point where, as an adult, we have a difficult time answering the simple question: "Who am I?" Let's explore that.

CONSIDER THE REFRESHING THREE-YEAR-OLD. When he entered school at age six, he really enjoyed wearing red cowboy boots. These boots were a birthday gift from Grandpa and were special. All the other kids, however, wore white Nikes. Feeling out of place and wanting acceptance, the child dumped those special red cowboy boots and showed up at school in his white Nikes. He had begun the process of moving away from the Real Me and into new territory called a "Facade." The Facade mode felt unnatural and unlike him, yet his will for acceptance exceeded his will for uniqueness.

In high school, he talked with his guidance counselor about his interest in art as a major. The counselor said, "You don't want to be an artist. There is no financial future in art. And besides, artists are flaky people. What you really want to be is a computer systems analyst." So the boy enrolled in computer classes—and another part of his essence closed off. That choice moved him farther from the Real Me mode and closer to the Facade mode.

As a young adult, he met that special person who seemed like an ideal mate. She was particularly attracted to his sensitivity—an unusual quality for a man. After several years of marriage, however, a different message came from his wife: "You are so *sensitive!* Why can't you be stronger like other men?" Sensitivity, the quality in him she originally had appreciated, now became a source of conflict. And the young man chose to move **149** farther from his Real Me mode. The Facade mode now took on a life of its own as his Real Me continued to be suppressed.

No wonder some people have difficulty with their identity. Each challenge of the Real Me is a choice point that has significant long-term implications. The composite of all these choice points is who we become and how we approach life. As this example illustrates, our choices sometimes result in our transitioning to a Facade mode.

Condition 2: Facade-to-Facade Communication

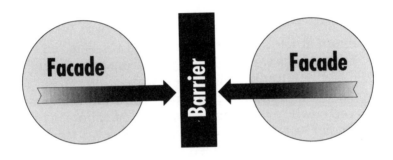

Condition 2 illustrates two people functioning in their Facade mode with a barrier between them. Facade-to-Facade communication is the most difficult and complex type. Neither of these people feel safe being themselves, and each therefore promotes an unreal image. A job applicant's résumé may demonstrate this point. The résumé presents only one-half of the balance sheet—the candidate's strengths. Not mentioned is the fact that she had four stormy divorces and a recent hospitalization for alcoholism, and has declared bankruptcy twice. Reading the résumé and talking with references who were carefully selected by the candidate might cause the interviewer to conclude that the applicant walks on water! No hint of weaknesses or liabilities is even suggested. Clearly the candidate presents a biased perspective while operating in her Facade mode.

The company interviewer may also operate from the Facade mode. Feeling that the candidate is a good fit for employment, the interviewer wants to assure that she joins the company. Moving into his Facade mode, the interviewer paints a glowing picture of the organization. He emphasizes salary and benefits, promotional opportunities, and the desirability of the community for her family. The interviewer does not mention that the company is in serious financial trouble, that the applicant's prospective boss is almost impossible to work for, and that five people have been in the position over the last eighteen months. Four months after being hired, the candidate realizes that she has made a terrible mistake. Her brief experience has not matched her expectations of the company at all. Her boss is a "beast" and management has announced curtailment of benefits and a salary freeze. Layoffs are just around the corner. The interviewer has also concluded that the new employee is not a good fit. A number of interpersonal conflicts have already happened between the new employee and several of her co-workers. Even three clients have registered complaints about her abrupt manner.

Facade-to-Facade communication often has little to do with reality. "Truth" seems to be situational while values and principles are put aside to meet expedient needs. Images become more important than substance. Energy and creativity are directed toward communicating what the current audience wants to hear. The Real Me becomes more distant as the speaker struggles to remember what was said to whom. Integrity and self-esteem ultimately suffer. Operating in the Facade mode leaves oneself and others less than whole.

Condition 3: "Real Me"-to-"Real Me" Communication

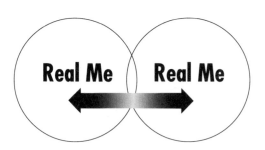

Condition 3 reflects quality, caring straight talk between individuals. For a moment, bring to mind your very best friend. Picture that person clearly and reflect on the nature and quality of your communication. Chances are, you can be yourself with that friend and still be accepted. Communication is open, safe, direct, and caring. There are no hidden agendas, no images to live up to, no baggage and barriers, no having to remember what you said in previous conversations. You simply tell the truth to one another. Notice the ease of communication.

In communicating Real Me to Real Me, people speak the truth without feeling the need to protect themselves. Because it provides mutual safety, shooting straight requires little courage. People connect in a joining of spirits as each empowers the other. Self-esteem is honored while each person remains whole and functions with integrity. Nurturing, healing, growing, and empowering result from relating Real Me to Real Me.

Condition 4: "Real Me"-to-Facade Communication

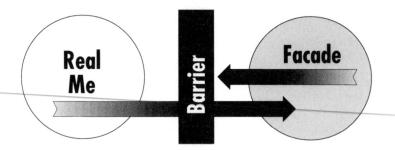

Condition 4 presents a special challenge: One person is in the Real Me mode and the other is in a Facade mode. The principle of courage and safety comes into sharp focus in this condition. Because we cannot *not* influence others, each person will have an impact. An opportunity exists for barriers to either remain or come down. The person who is functioning in the Facade mode feels unsafe and may have old relationship baggage that continues to get in the way. Punching through the barrier requires both safety and courage. Even if conditions are safe, insufficient courage will keep the individual from crossing the barrier.

The person who is willing to function in the Real Me mode can assist the other by providing emotional safety. Seeking understanding, telling the truth, listening, pausing, looking for points of agreement, and focusing on interests rather than positions are all important strategies in punching through barriers.

At some point, the person in the Facade mode may be sufficiently influenced by the person in the Real Me mode to take a leap of faith and break through the barrier. Conditions are most vulnerable at this moment. The leap of faith requires immediate encouragement—even if the behavior lacks skill or the comments seem out of line. Rewarding movement rather than criticizing unskilled behavior encourages continued growth. As the barriers decline, communicating Real Me to Real Me begins to take on new substance. Once they have experienced the sweet taste of this type of communication, people are unlikely to return to the shallow depths of Facade-to-Facade exchanges.

When consulting with groups in which people have dysfunctional communication and large amounts of baggage, I role model being in the Real Me mode while providing safety. Through advance work, I usually am familiar with their barriers, stuck points, and baggage. With rare exceptions, I am privileged to assist people in punching through their "stuff." By creating a genuine experience of communicating Real Me to Real Me and building skills to support these new behaviors, I help groups learn how to make the transition from dysfunctional exchanges to caring straight talk. Coupled with the concept of accountability and the spirit of partnership, a sense of growth and renewal encourages individuals to continue their efforts in making a positive difference. Increased awareness provides these individuals with new choice points.

"There is only one fear; the fear of not being able to cope."

Will Schutz   **153**

In a workshop taught by Gay and Kathlyn Hendricks, authors of the book *Conscious Loving* (1990), they referred to the Facade mode as a "persona" and the Real Me mode as our "essence." When we are in our essence, we are conscious, aware, present, and centered. The essence state can be interrupted by a significant emotional event or we can slowly become counterproductive through lack of awareness and self-correction. When we do not express our feelings truthfully, we shift to a persona or Facade mode as a way to protect ourselves. Perhaps some of the following Facade or persona modes, as described by both Gay and Kathlyn Hendricks and Gary Koyen, might be familiar:

Facade Roles

Charmer	Rebel	Martyr
Caretaker	Clown	Perfectionist
Critic	Bulldozer	Drama queen or king
Professor	Skeptic	Mr. or Ms. "nice guy"
Judge	Pleaser	Airhead
Chameleon	Trouper	Loner
Rescuer	Blamer	Stoic
Workaholic	Victim	Addict

Which are your favorites? Rather than functioning in your essence or Real Me mode, to which of the above Facades do you experience behavioral attachments? By staying in touch with the Real Me, we think of ourselves as beings who have feelings and Facades. Through fear and not being able to cope with difficult life experiences, we are driven to the point of "becoming" our Facades. In this state, we protect ourselves from working through our insecurities.

When we function in our Facade mode, we tend to attract people who live within their Facade mode. The "Perfectionist" may attract the "Airhead," enabling each to "shine" in his or her own Facade mode. They view each other and communicate through their respective "Facade filters." Positive energy diminishes as relationship tension increases.

By getting to know our true identity, by accepting that we are already lovable and capable, we lose our need to live in a pretend state. Choosing illusion rather than the truth avoids short-term pain, yet it prevents us from experiencing life to its fullest. The way out is through, and the way through requires caring straight talk.

In the Facade mode, we are unconscious and on automatic pilot. Stuck-state conditions immediately surface. We don't have to think creatively or deal with uncomfortable issues. Conversely, we can be "right" and in control, and we can avoid being controlled by external forces.

The costs of being in the Facade mode require careful examination. Instead of experiencing the vibrancy and joy of life, we separate ourselves from our feelings and become numb. Exploration of the self is blocked as interpersonal connection becomes stilted, and creativity shifts from positive application to protecting ourselves while blaming others. We get to stay stuck in our stuff. This deenergizing experience detracts from our self-esteem and the esteem of others. Perhaps even more significant costs include the loss of genuine creative expression and of our connection with ourself and others.

> ## "To be, or not to be: that is the question."
> William Shakespeare

Joy, enlightenment, prosperity, and quality relationships are not experienced in the Facade mode. In the Real Me or essence state of being, however, these elements become vibrant. Telling the "microscopic truth," which Gay and Kathlyn Hendricks define as the area that "absolutely cannot be argued about," enables us to connect with ourself and others. When we take full responsibility for being aware of and expressing our feelings (of being sad, mad, glad, and afraid), we have a vehicle for building quality relationships at work and home. "Telling the truth pops the cork," according to Will Schutz (1979), and "out flows the real person." As people unfold, aliveness and energy results.

AWARENESS CHECKS

- Where in your life are you functioning in a Facade mode? At work? At home?

- What payoffs are you receiving for functioning in this state?

- What short-term and long-term costs might you experience?

- What if you became the "real me" at home and work?

- What is the learning?

Care enough to tell your truth—and receive others' truth—with clarity and acceptance. In the long run, you will have fewer surprise wake-up calls. Experience the difference in your relationships, starting within yourself, when you tell your truth as a lifestyle rather than as a specific strategy. Commitment to sharing your truth and being open to hearing the truth of others provides a foundation for quality relationships and long-term growth. Committing to straight talk becomes the difference that makes a difference. Commit to aliveness through your truth.

"When in doubt, tell the truth."

Mark Twain

CHAPTER

15

Linking Courage with Safety:
EXCHANGING TRUTH

*". . . the truth shall make
you free."*

John 8:32

"We just can't communicate" is a
far too common statement in
personal and professional settings. Perhaps a more accountable assessment
might be either "I am not committed to
do what it takes to communicate well in
this relationship" or "I have not developed my communication skills sufficiently to deal with this situation."
Effective communication requires both
intent and *skills*. Choosing to communicate well and refining communicative

157

skills positions us to experience greater understanding and more fulfilling relationships.

"All things are difficult before they are easy."
John Norley

Communication is simply a vehicle for understanding through giving and receiving feedback. The following key elements are required to enhance the quality of interpersonal communication:

1. Demonstrate *courage* both in self-disclosing and in giving straight, caring feedback.

2. Provide *safety* by making it easy for others to give you both positive and negative feedback.

It's that simple—courage and safety! Yet we often make the communication process so complicated! Talking straight requires courage in sharing two dimensions: (1) our internal experience—what we are thinking, feeling, and wanting; and (2) our feedback to others regarding what is going well and what is not going well. Rather than exercising timely courage, we often withhold it and allow the piles to get beyond the manageable stage. Or the emotional baggage accumulates so that when we finally "get it off our chest," the *way* in which we express our internal frustration damages our relationships.

Providing safety to others in receiving feedback facilitates healthy and timely communication. Feedback helps us to increase self-awareness, grow, address issues needing attention, identify blind spots, reinforce strengths, discover hidden talents, and build relationships. Encouraging and rewarding both positive and negative feedback provides emotional safety to others. Both affirming and constructive feedback are gifts. Safety encourages timely feedback while creating a nurturing climate for quality relationships. When we combine courage and safety in the communication process, we achieve exciting results! Let's explore the application of these concepts both personally and professionally.

I AM REMINDED OF THE STORY of Captain Gerald Coffee, a pilot in the U.S. Navy who was shot down and captured during the Vietnam War. During his seven years and nine days as a prisoner of war, he and the other Americans at the "Hanoi Hilton" were forbidden to communicate with one another. If they were caught talking, severe punishment resulted. Conditions could not have been poorer for effective communication. Yet the POWs had a clear *intent* to communicate and to relate to one another.

The POWs developed a creative alphabet code system consisting of knocks tapped out on their isolation cell walls. Messages leapfrogged from cell to cell. Church service, conducted each Sunday morning through a series of coded knocks, inspired prisoners. When a prisoner was removed from a cell for torture, "GB" or "God bless" sounded through walls as a source of reassurance and support. The coded taps communicated: "We are with you—hang in there!"

During their rare outdoor exercise opportunities, the POWs continued their creative methods of communicating with one another, even under hostile conditions. Folding their arms, scratching their face, spitting—each gesture communicated a secret message undetected by the prison guards. Yet the messages got through. The POWs had a clear intent to communicate and converted this intent into courageous action! These prisoners of war would have a difficult time understanding someone who claims, "We just cannot communicate."

With intent, we can communicate.

In many respects, communication skills are far less important than the simple intent to communicate. When we travel in foreign countries, for example, numerous opportu- **159** nities arise to communicate with people who do not even share a common language with us. The *intent* to communicate transcends skill levels and even language "barriers"; human beings demonstrate remarkable communication versatility in accomplishing their interests. Coupling intent with enhanced communication skills, however, results in quality communication that can make a profound difference.

Communication barriers have little to do with skill levels and shared language. More often than not, communication "blocks" reflect relationship tension in the form of low trust levels, sensitive history, unmet expectations, distorted perceptions, hurt feelings, fear of intimacy, unresolved conflict, low self-esteem, and a low propensity for risk taking. Caring straight talk tends to reduce rather than intensify communication blocks. Communication barriers seldom get in the way—relationship issues do. The way out of these issues is not around, but through. Communication becomes the vehicle, not the barrier.

There are three communication styles:

1. *Passive:* Indirect, soft on issues, soft on people, and potentially crazymaking

2. *Aggressive:* Straight, tough on issues, tough on people, and potentially damaging

3. *Assertive:* Straight, tough on issues, soft on people, and affirming

Passive Communication

Passive communication dances around the truth and forces the listener to interpret messages, signs, and signals. For example, one might say, "If he really loved me, he would know what I want and feel." While the statement may contain an element of inherent truth, passive communication requires the listener to play games and guess about the speaker's internal experience. Messages are often indirect, confusing, and crazymaking! Relationship stress intensifies, further complicating the communication process and detracting from intimacy and closeness. Passive communication undermines trust, encourages assumptions, and lacks both courage and safety.

If passive communication is practiced for a long time, significant relationship surprises or wake-up calls can be expected. If, for example, a husband withholds his truth (what he is really thinking, feeling, and wanting), his wife is likely to experience blind spots. His inability to share these important inner states eventually erodes the relationship and causes both partners to shut down. Additionally, the growth of the individual and the couple is limited, since each ultimately lives within his or her respective comfort zone. An entanglement develops as quality relating subsides.

Consider these examples of passive communication and the suggested interpretations:

Passive Communication

Passive Statement:	Hidden Meaning:
Nothing's wrong!"	"I feel frustrated and angry."
"I don't care where we go for dinner."	"I would enjoy Chinese food."
"You're doing a fine job."	"I have concerns about . . ."
"That makes sense to me."	"I see it differently."
"Don't trouble yourself with the coffee."	"I would love a cup of coffee."

Passive communication withholds feelings, wants, and thoughts. Principles are avoided as one person appears to agree with another while putting aside his or her personal feelings and values. As a result of indirect statements, frequent apologies, and hedging, the listener takes on the task of guessing about the speaker's internal state. Fear and self-esteem issues are often at the root of passive communication. As with most dysfunctional human behavior, empathetic listening requires us to recognize that each of us does the best we know how, given our level of awareness.

161

Quality relating requires the direct expression of important wants and needs. Bottled-up feelings, on the other hand, tend to create resentment, resulting in fault finding, criticism, periodic emotional outbreaks, and other forms of relationship tension. Both self-respect and intimacy diminish. The timely, direct expression of feelings, wants, needs, and expectations, on the other hand, establishes a positive framework for building relationships. Passive communication, especially when it is used to avoid important issues, generates conditions that lead to significant wake-up calls. Choosing to talk straight generates far better results than allowing "stuff" to accumulate.

Passive communication can be useful, however, in some circumstances. When an issue is of low importance to you and high importance to someone else, accommodating works well. When others are in a sensitive state, when conflict occurs in an unimportant relationship, or when calming others is essential, passive communication produces acceptable results. Applying this communication style appropriately assists in building rapport and connecting with others.

Aggressive Communication

Aggressive communication is potentially harmful straight talk. Although the point gets across and the "truth" gets told, the listener may be damaged in the process.

SOME YEARS AGO, I WAS CONDUCTING a three-day communication seminar for executives at a hotel. On the second day, several hotel workers approached me during a seminar break and told me how much they appreciated the courteous way the people in my seminar were treating the employees. While I agreed with their observation, I was curious about what had caused them to come to that conclusion. Only the week before, a seminar titled "Assertiveness Training for Women," with 250 participants, was conducted in that same hotel. The seminar leader encouraged participants to practice their "assertiveness" on the hotel workers during the session. At lunch, for example, women demanded of the waiters: "You—get over here! This meat is not cooked well enough. I am paying good money for this lunch and I deserve better. Now take it back to the kitchen and bring me food that's cooked properly!"

For three days, seminar participants practiced what they thought were assertive communication techniques on the hotel workers. Instead, they were learning and practicing *aggressive* communication strategies. Sensitivity to the human element was absent. Can you imagine how the waiters, housekeepers, and receptionists felt as recipients of this group communication experiment? A collective sigh of relief rolled through the hallways when the group finally left. Immediately, however, a new sign went up on the meeting marquee announcing my three-day communication seminar. When they saw that, the hotel workers braced themselves for more badgering and battering. Their experience with the participants in my seminar turned out to be far different—and pleasant. They experienced caring straight talk.

Aggressive communication attempts to control situations through practices that range from a loud, cold voice and pointing finger to stern glares and icy silence. This style does not work well when it is used as a power play, when the issue is of little importance, when you can't afford to make another enemy, or when you lock out other options too soon and rigidly defend a narrow point of view. Aggressive communication is long on courage and short on safety.

Aggressive communication can be appropriate, however, in several circumstances. When the issue or principle is of high importance to you and other efforts at communication have not been effective, becoming more aggressive may produce better results. A more aggressive position may be the best strategy in response to aggressive communication or when the assertive approach has not gotten through. Be careful, however, not to inflame the situation. An "I win, you lose" solution may just be temporary, causing the other person to "keep score" for future retaliation purposes. Creating a "win-lose" situation usually sets the stage for a long-term "lose-lose" situation.

163

Assertive Communication

Straight talk, or assertive communication, involves telling our truth in a caring way. By separating the person from the issue or behavior, we set the stage for mutual understanding and meeting shared needs. Caring straight talk fosters respect for oneself and others while directly addressing issues. Speaking assertively facilitates acceptance of feelings and perceptions, even when perspectives differ. Additionally, caring straight talk encourages people to make changes when appropriate; it exercises courage while providing safety.

Like the other communication styles, assertive communication has some drawbacks. Your "authenticity" may contribute to unnecessary conflict or may focus on issues that are not very important in the grand scheme of things. In unimportant relationships, the benefits of shooting straight may not be worth the energy required. Some years ago, my two sons and I were on a long drive and stopped at a Mexican restaurant for dinner. The food was terrible! We filled up on chips and water, leaving most of the main course. Because I was tired and anxious to get home, I did not want to deal with the issue of their poor-quality food. As we left, the hostess asked, "How was your food?" Since accountability and telling the truth are important principles in our family, both sons riveted their eyes on me, waiting to see how I would handle this. I responded, "It was filling!" When we walked to the car, my oldest son said to me, "Dad—it was *filling?*" Somehow, he did not buy my approach! However, putting energy into a restaurant that we would never see again was not worth the effort.

Straight talk matches our outer expression with our inner experience.

Straight talk is a *caring* approach to understanding through matching our outer expression (what we say) with our inner experience (what we are thinking, wanting, and

STRAIGHT TALK

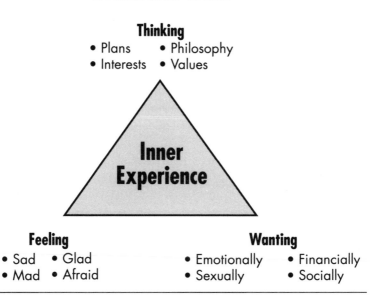

Thinking
- Plans
- Philosophy
- Interests
- Values

Inner Experience

Feeling
- Sad
- Glad
- Mad
- Afraid

Wanting
- Emotionally
- Financially
- Sexually
- Socially

feeling). Refer to the straight-talk diagram and note the inner experience "communication triangle." Of the three elements, which is the most comfortable to share at home and at work: thinking, feeling, or wanting? The majority of people experience the greatest ease in sharing what they are thinking, then what they are wanting, and last what they are feeling. What is least comfortable tends to be withheld.

When we withhold communication, our partner, work associate, or child must guess about our unexpressed inner experiences. Having to guess about what others are thinking, feeling, and wanting contributes to relationship tension. Completed communication requires us to accurately express, in a caring way, our feelings, thoughts, and wants. What elements do you resist sharing, and what consequences do you experience?

According to recent studies, the average American adult spends fewer than fifteen minutes per day in quality communication with his or her spouse and less than four minutes per day communicating with his or her children. Such limited quantity **165** impairs the quality of communication. The development of rapport, safety, and courage in communication is unlikely with such limited exchanges. To what extent have you behaviorally committed to quality communication in your important relationships? While it takes two to make a relationship, only one is required to change it.

Internationally, we "sever diplomatic relations" when another country does something we don't like. We expel their diplomats; they expel ours. We stop talking and close off communication channels at the very moment when diplomatic efforts should be expanded and intensified. Children who are angry with one another might say, "You made me mad, and I'm not going to talk with you anymore." Adults wouldn't accept such childish behavior, so instead we pursue the more sophisticated approach of "severing diplomatic relations." Both intentions and results are the same, however. International tensions increase and we bring out the "big guns" to "resolve" our differences.

The real test of your values is not when things are going well; the real test is when things are *not* going well. When relationship tension strikes, how do you handle communication? When the pressure is on at home or at work, do you expand and intensify communication efforts or "sever diplomatic relations"? In the process of talking straight, seeking first to understand the other person demonstrates respect while positioning them to be more open to understanding your thoughts, feelings, and wants. Communication under pressure can provide insight as to what both parties really value.

Care enough to communicate your feelings.

Of the three communication elements, most people are least likely to share feelings. And feelings that reflect relationship tension are like worms. Like *worms?* Have you ever tried to bury a worm? They thrive underground. Worms mate, multiply, and become even bigger after burial. And then they resurface, perhaps when you least expect them. You cannot bury a worm and expect it to remain underground. You cannot bury a feeling and expect it to remain underground. Buried feelings, especially those involving relationship issues, intensify as they link with other past resentments and unresolved conflicts. At the most inopportune time, stuffed feelings surface with escalated emotions.

Denying or burying feelings retards the life experience and significantly cripples relationships. Moreover, buried feelings have been implicated in nearly every form of human illness. The energy and resources that are ultimately committed to deal with passive communication far exceed what would have been required to work through the situation in the first place. Even though the short-term costs of straight talk appear to be high, choosing to express rather than repress feelings assists in building quality, long-term relationships. Examine your own commitment to truth:

AWARENESS CHECKS

- What feelings do you find easy to express?

- What feelings do you avoid experiencing?

- What things do you most often resist telling the truth about?

- When you are under stress or challenged, what happens to your truth?

- When you "settle for," what results do you experience?

- What is the learning?

167

SEVERAL YEARS AGO, WORKERS AT a U.S. auto manufacturing plant buried their feelings toward management. Resentment grew as they looked for creative ways to express their anger. A passive-aggressive solution surfaced—spot welding empty beer cans into the door panels of vehicles on the assembly line! Several months later, the spot weld would break, causing the can to fall down into the door panel and rattle. Consumers then complained to management about the quality of American cars. Assembly line workers "won" by getting management into trouble. What a "solution"! In recent years the American automotive market share has experienced a marked decline. Buried feelings can be costly.

Passive, aggressive, and assertive communication strategies are all choices. Each deals with the truth differently and generates a distinct outcome. Committing to straight talk demonstrates caring while producing even better results. When we allow communication to become sloppy, poor outcomes result. For a moment, examine the personal and professional contexts of your communication. In which environment do you exercise greater skill and care? In which environment do you communicate most effectively? What do you do differently to achieve those more satisfying results?

When you exercise courage in giving feedback, courage in disclosing your inner state, and safety in receiving feedback from others, you create an environment for quality communication. Care enough to connect your head and heart in the communication process. Care enough to be fully present in your communication with others and experience the freedom of truth.

16

Straight Talk:

DOIN' IT!

*"As my awareness increases, my control
over my own being increases."*

Will Schutz

So, how *do* we talk straight? Getting
straight with others requires that
we first get straight with ourselves—
that we be self-aware. Pausing before
communicating provides clarity and
positions *us* to load the process for
success. When we care enough to communicate well, we position the listener
to participate in the exchange process
with greater awareness, understanding,
and safety.

While two or more people are involved in any communication process,
only one is needed to alter the course to
higher consciousness. You are an influential role model in creating a *climate*
and *process* for effective communication. The straight-talk exchange starts
with you. When you set the standard,

Wake-Up Calls

others frequently choose to follow your lead. Choosing to be open, honest, direct, caring, and accountable is contagious.

Straight talk requires a conscious commitment to generate more favorable outcomes by communicating with integrity. Matching your external expression (what you say) with your internal experience (what you think, feel, and want) becomes an important strategy in building quality relations with others—and in building a stronger sense of self. Not a mere strategy, straight talk is a life choice.

When you are put to the test in a sensitive situation, how do you communicate? What does your behavior teach others about quality communication? If others follow your lead, where will you lead them regarding communicating with integrity? The result of your communication reflects your intent.

Straight-talk strategies are just that—strategies. Tools are of little value until they are put to use. Intention, coupled with applied skills, creates a difference that makes a difference. Getting straight first with ourselves provides internal clarity while positioning others to join us in a caring straight-talk exchange.

An argument can be made that straight-talk strategies take the spontaneity out of the communication process. Actually, the opposite results. When co-workers or family members learn to count on you to talk straight and listen actively, they feel free to be themselves. They have no reason to protect themselves, look for hidden agendas, or hide their inner experiences. Through your conscious commitment to talking straight and providing safety, a secure environment is created for spontaneous, real communication. Communication becomes the vehicle for building quality relations.

Application of the following communication guidelines can prepare us for more favorable communication outcomes:

COMMUNICATION GUIDELINES

Loading the Process for Success

1. *Why* do I want to communicate?
   - Intentions or purpose?
   - Desired outcomes?

2. *What* do I want to communicate?
   - Contents?
   - Feelings?

3. *When* could communication be most effective?
   - Now?
   - Later?

4. *Where* could communication be most effective?
   - "My place?"
   - "Your place?"
   - Neutral territory?

5. *How* could communication be most effective?
   - Building understanding?
   - Building relationships?

Internal clarification of *why* we want to communicate positions us to transfer that same clarity to the listener. Being clear about intentions and outcomes facilitates the listener to join rather than resist. Clarity of direction and clean intentions provides safety, in contrast to mixed messages, which discourage trust and openness.

What we communicate, including content and feelings, expedites understanding. Matching content and feelings enables the listener to more accurately interpret our intended messages.

Timing, or *when* we communicate, significantly affects the quality of our interactions. In most cases, communicating immediately after or close to the triggering event keeps relationships current and healthy. "Shovel while the piles are small" becomes a wise strategy in building quality relationships.

Where one communicates important messages can contribute to or detract from intended results. Some messages are best shared privately, while others achieve their intended results in a more public environment. Sitting on the same side of a conference table in "neutral" territory may work best in one sensitive situation, while communicating in your office and sitting behind your desk might better serve another need. Never select the bed as a place for negative discussions or arguments with your partner. Get out of bed for those talks. A bed is for two purposes, and arguing is not one of them!

How we communicate often influences the outcome even more than what we actually have to say. Recall a time when someone might have said to you, "It's not *what* you said, but *how* you said it that bothered me." Care enough to select words that accurately reflect your message and feelings. Additionally, committing in advance to building a relationship—and following through with that commitment—makes a significant and positive difference. A positive intention more than compensates for low skill levels in the communication process.

Be tough on issues and soft on people.

Practicing the principle of being tough on issues and soft on people allows you to deal directly with difficult problems while remaining sensitive to the human element. Roger Fisher and William Ury, authors of *Getting to Yes* (1983), encourage this strategy as a means of talking straight while keeping people present. Separating people from the problem provides safety while minimizing defensiveness, rationalization, and self-justification. We can talk straight without damaging people or relationships.

The following guidelines will help you to be tough on issues and soft on people:

GUIDELINES FOR GIVING FEEDBACK

Demonstrate the courage to:

1. Clarify your intentions to yourself and others.
2. Tailor feedback to the individual.

3. Give feedback close to the triggering event.

4. Be specific and descriptive.

5. Assert while affirming.

   • Assert (state thoughts, feelings, wants)

   • Affirm (be respectful and caring)

6. Focus on actions or behavior, not the actor or person.

7. Pause and check for understanding.

"We are not our tapes."

Ken Keyes

Ken Keyes described a superb strategy for being tough on issues and soft on people. In a relationship seminar he conducted, Keyes said, "We are not our tapes!" He demonstrated this principle by referring to a portable cassette tape player. The cassette player has the flexibility to play an infinite variety of tapes. With blind obedience, the player perfectly reproduces whatever is programmed on the tape. The cassette machine itself merely does what the tape commands. If the music coming from the speakers doesn't match our taste, we don't discard the tape player. The cassette machine is just fine. We need to change tapes, not junk the recorder.

As human beings, we have great potential and enormous flexibility. When the results in a given situation do not serve us, the problem relates to our tape selection. Like the cassette player, we are just fine. The tapes we choose, however, often get in our way. We are not our tapes—we *select* our tapes. When we pause at our choice points, increase our awareness, and select behavioral tapes that better serve us, our lives will begin to hum!

I HAD AN OPPORTUNITY TO APPLY this concept in a difficult situation with my stepson. When he was a young teenager, he **173** stole some money and covered up his misdeed with a series of "white lies." I was angry with his poor choices and struggled to apply these principles! Fortunately, I remembered to pause. As a parent, I was confronted with having to hold him accountable (tough on issues), yet be compassionate (soft on people). I needed to talk straight, respect him as an individual, and assist him in making more accountable choices. A tall order!

In our family, "life school" sessions are occasionally held where we discuss wake-up calls and choice points. This was one of those times. I asked him to come into my room and bring his cassette player and two tapes. With a look of confusion, he asked, "Any tapes in particular?" "No, just two tapes." I sat down with the cassette player in my lap and said, "When you don't like the music playing from this machine, you don't throw the cassette player away. The machine is OK. The tape is the problem. When garbage music comes out of the cassette player, remove the tape from the machine and replace it with one that serves you better." At that point, I pulled the tape out of the machine, tossed it across the room, and replaced it with another one.

Still confused, he replied that he did not understand where this "life school" session was leading. I then said to him, "You, like this cassette player, are OK. The tapes of stealing and lying, however, are not OK. As an honor student and musician, many things are going well in your life. Yet these specific tapes, your choices to lie and steal, are totally unacceptable! I am going to ask you a number of questions about this incident, and I want the absolute truth. If you choose not to tell me the truth, I will choose to see to it that charges are brought against you. I care for you, yet these behaviors must change!"

He no longer looked confused. He got the point that he was OK, but his specific behaviors were not acceptable. A new, significant choice point was at hand. He could either be accountable and tell me the truth or continue playing the tapes that got him into trouble. After pausing for a moment, he chose to shoot straight by answering a number of tough questions related to the theft. His accountability made a difference for both of us.

This was perhaps the most difficult incident we experienced in our relationship. Both of us cried and hugged each other as we worked through this tough process. We later met with the individual from whom the money had been stolen and developed a repayment plan for which my stepson was totally responsible. I was pleased with how open and accountable he chose to be in what had to be a tough situation for him. The choices he made following this wake-up call became an important turning point in his life.

As I drove my stepson to a friend's house about a week later, he said to me, "Eric, I am really glad you are in my life." Considering the sometimes difficult relationship between a stepson and stepfather, this statement meant a great deal to me. Application of the principle of being tough on issues and soft on people established a new and positive dimension in our relationship.

Separate the person from the problem.

What if your boss, in a performance evaluation, has just completed a discussion of your strengths and then says, "Now, let's talk about your weaknesses"? The chances are that your internal response might be defensive, cautious, argumentative, or fearful. When you feel threatened, quality communication is unlikely to take place. On the other hand, what if your boss says, "Let's explore ideas that will enable you to be even more effective. What could you do more of and less of that would contribute to your effectiveness?" Focusing on "stretches" rather than weaknesses provides greater communication safety and invites the other person to join rather than resist exploration of performance issues.

When you give difficult or sensitive feedback to others, asserting your interests while simultaneously affirming them as a person assists in producing positive results. Assertiveness focuses on the issues and communicates your feelings, wants, and thoughts. Affirming demonstrates respect and caring for someone else by separating behaviors from the individual. Careful attention should be given to acknowledging the person's **175** *strengths* or "well dones," as well as to working through the *stretches* or opportunities for improvement. Some say that these terms are mere semantics, yet most people respond well to this encouraging and supportive approach. Exploration of "weaknesses" and "shortcomings" often precipitates defensive responses, while concentrating on "stretches" directs creative energy to problem solving and results. While they are not ignored, negative issues are addressed with caring openness. Such respectful straight talk encourages others to join rather than resist in the problem-solving process.

Straight talk: a three-step strategy.

Straight talk consists of three steps:

1. This is what I *experienced.*

2. This is how I *feel.*

3. This is what I *want.*

An example will demonstrate the use of these steps in practice.

SOME YEARS AGO, A CORPORATE EXECUTIVE asked me to work with one of the company's regional presidents, who was experiencing considerable difficulty in relating to her leadership team. After several direct telephone conversations, I flew to her East Coast office for the purpose of enhancing team relationships and communication. I interviewed each of her key leadership-team members and found a disturbing behavioral pattern. They all were concerned that when they talked with her, she frequently reacted with screaming and accusations. Communication shut down as they retreated to safety rather than being subjected to her tirades. Clearly, a tough mission.

After completing interviews with her team, I met with her for the purpose of giving feedback and planning the next steps

in the intervention process. Starting with her strengths, I summarized what I had learned was going well. She received this news with pleasure and was most attentive.

Shifting gears to stretches or opportunities for improvement, I shared the information that her staff would like her to increase her active listening, pause more, provide more affirming feedback, express more clarity of direction, and be more accessible. Conversely, she could enhance her effectiveness by demonstrating less premature closure, less criticizing of individuals in front of others, less elevating of her voice when she disagreed, less . . . I was not able to finish. She stood up, put her hands on her hips, and started screaming at me, "I am sick and tired of hearing this! I do not scream at others, and I do not criticize people!" Even though we were behind closed doors, her voice carried down the hall of the executive suite as she screamed at me. I later learned that a small crowd gathered outside her office and concluded, "Eric is getting it now!" And I was.

When the wind died down, I said to her, "Can I give you some feedback?" Her eyes narrowed, and she guardedly said, "Yes." At that point, I took a deep breath, paused for a head-heart connection, and applied the three-step straight-talk strategy:

> What I just experienced [step 1] mirrors what your staff said about how you deal with stress. Your elevated voice and position standing over me matches the very concerns they expressed. What you are doing right now with me is the very thing they fear most from you. And rather than take a chance on this happening, they choose to withdraw and withhold. The communication then tends to be guarded and unsafe.
>
> Right now, I feel [step 2] angry and intimidated. I want to close my briefcase, climb back on the plane, and fly home. This is not fun, and frankly I do not choose to be the object of these kinds of behaviors.
>
> What I want [step 3] is to be able to work with you in a mutually respectful way that produces good long-term results for you, your organization, and me. Right now, you are at an important choice point. If you choose to treat me the way you just did, I have no interest in continuing this business relationship. If you choose to openly explore these issues, I will do everything I can to assist you in producing positive results.

177

When she heard this, she became very quiet. I then asked, "What if you continue this kind of interaction with your staff?" After reflecting for a moment, she softly said, "I will get fired." I agreed. Another choice point. "So where do we go from here?" I asked. She said, "If you are willing to work with me, I want to deal with this. I have similar relationship issues at home and need to do something differently." She punched through an important resistance barrier with that insight, and we began our work. That became the first of many barriers she punched through in the following months on her journey to new awareness.

Expressing what you experienced, how you feel, and what you want provides clarity to yourself and others—and gets to the heart of the issue. Rather than describing some behavior that occurred in the past, far greater understanding can be derived from focusing on the current experience. The president's elevated voice and standing position felt intimidating. The straight-talk feedback I gave to her related to my experience at that moment. And she was then able to make the connection between her behaviors and my feelings. The immediate feedback I delivered assisted her in transforming her behaviors by making more aware, conscious choices. Timely straight talk provided the vehicle to make that positive difference.

Think of a time when you gave difficult feedback to an individual and he responded by saying, "Give me an example!" Being careful not to offend him, you carefully described a past situation. He then reacted with anger, rationalizing, defending, and justifying his position, and said, "Give me another example!" Perhaps more timidly you accommodated his request with yet another example of intimidating or insensitive behavior. At that point, he become incensed, ripped your example to pieces, and discredited you. Now what?

The situation could not be more perfect! What he is doing *right now* duplicates his past behavioral problems. Past examples are not even needed. The present-moment experience is far more relevant and powerful in communicating what you experience, what you feel, and what you want. This teachable moment or wake-up call provides a window of opportunity. Seize

178

the moment by providing straight, caring feedback to him regarding your current experience; for example:

> In this current conversation, each example I offer is challenged. I am feeling frustrated, anxious, and angry. It doesn't feel safe to give you feedback under these circumstances, and your behavior right now appears to match the very concerns I was attempting to describe in the examples. I want us to have a free and open exchange of caring feedback. I am going to double my active listening efforts and invite you to join me in doing the same.

When you describe what you have experienced, be sure to use objective rather than emotionally charged or accusatory language. Calling someone a "jerk" will only inflame the situation and damage the relationship. An attack on the person tends to escalate relationship stress and encourage retaliation.

When you give feedback, separate the behavior from the individual. Rather than slur the person, focus on the issue; for example:

> When you criticized my work in front of my peers yesterday, I felt embarrassed. I want and value your feedback, and I have learned much from your advice. I want you to continue giving me feedback, but I prefer that critical feedback be given to me privately. That works much better for me while making it easy for you as well.

Treat others the way **they** *want to be treated.*

Gaining rapport with others assists in building effective relationships and facilitates straight talk. Our ability to adapt to others and deal effectively with various relationships has much to do with the "how" dimension of talking straight. Trust and credibility in relationships follow from our flexibility and versatility.

179

An interpretation of the Golden Rule suggests that you treat others the way you want to be treated. That works fine if they are like you, and not so fine if they are different. You run the risk of treating people inappropriately from their perspective and imposing your value system on them. Instead of "chemistry," conflict is likely to occur, according to Jim Cathcart and Tony Alessandra in their *Relationship Strategies* audiotapes (1984).

The spirit of the Golden Rule suggests a different approach: "Treat others the way *they* want to be treated." This approach establishes rapport, expands interpersonal comfort zones, and increases trust and credibility; interpersonal chemistry occurs as you are positioned to influence others with integrity.

Behavioral versatility may appear to be manipulative in nature. The *intent,* however, determines the outcome. If the intent is to get others to do something at their expense for your benefit, the negative manipulation will increase relationship tension. If positive relationship strategies are approached with a win-win intent, however, they can augment your ability to influence others while enhancing relationships.

Behavioral versatility focuses on what you do to yourself, not what you do to others. Versatility is a process of building rapport by adjusting your directness, style, and pace to match the other person's preference. While continuing to honor who you are, versatility enables you to tap into the internal resources offered by your less frequently used talents. A win-win outcome is more likely to follow these straight, yet flexible, behaviors.

In neurolinguistic terms, this behavioral versatility process is referred to as "match/pace/lead." Matching and pacing build rapport. Once we are in rapport, then we can lead or influence. Not establishing rapport, however, results in resistance or relationship tension. Resistance generally tells us that we are not in rapport and therefore need to adjust our directness, style, and pace to ease tension. Developing rapport provides safety and facilitates straight talk between the speaker and the listener.

The "Ugly American" syndrome provides an example of failure to build rapport through matching and pacing. *Matching* in foreign travel requires being aware of and sensitive to the different cultures, styles, norms, values, and language we encounter. "When in Rome, do as the Romans do" captures the meaning of matching. *Pacing* requires us to adjust our speed to the pace of others. For example, we might increase our pace with people from New York or Rome and slow our pace with people from Birmingham or London. If attempts to lead are made without matching and pacing, resistance results; if matching and pacing are used effectively, rapport occurs. We can then lead or influence with integrity.

Having done substantial research over the past dozen years on personality styles, I have seen clear patterns emerge that can assist you in communicating effectively. Honoring differences, like honoring the cultures of foreign countries, facilitates rapport building. The way others act toward you usually reflects how you act toward them. Your ability to adapt to others and deal effectively with relationships is a function of versatility, which involves awareness, sensitivity, and a knowledge of appropriate responses. If you apply a higher level of match/pace/lead communication skills and treat others the way they want to be treated, you will see rapport develop. Explore the following matching and pacing strategies for behavioral styles developed in my research since 1980:

Analyzing Behavioral Style Preference.   Match by being organized, thorough, and practical. Support logic and structure while communicating unemotionally. Avoid pressuring, spontaneous change, and high risks. Maintain a slow and steady pace, giving the analyzer adequate time to process thoughts.

Controlling Behavioral Style Preference.   Match by being direct, efficient, and result-oriented. Appeal to challenge while giving latitude. Avoid wasting time, making excuses, and indecision. Pace by being fast, getting to the point *now,* and focusing on results.

Supporting Behavioral Style Preference.   Match by being sincere, personal, and empathetic. Support others' principles and values while communicating sincerely. Avoid injustice, impa- **181**

tience, apathy, and betrayal. Maintain a relatively slow pace while appealing to causes and ideals.

Promoting Behavioral Style Preference.   Match by being personable, stimulating, and accepting. Support others' dreams, creativity, and ambitions. Avoid detail, being boring, and moving too slowly. Interact at a fast pace while providing recognition and admiration.

Application of the match/pace/lead concept in work and home relationships assists in creating a safe, open environment for caring straight talk. Like foreign countries, each person has a unique culture, style, and pace. Matching with task-oriented people requires getting right to the point, focusing on results, and minimizing physical contact and social interaction. Matching with relationship-oriented people may be less direct, yet more open. Sharing feelings, showing warmth, and being personable also assist in building rapport with a relationship-oriented person. With fast-paced, quick-thinking people, we need to talk, move, and decide at a faster rate. With slower-paced styles, rapport is achieved by talking, moving, and deciding at a slower rate; listening more; and reducing energy levels.

Matching and pacing build rapport while facilitating straight talk. Because we go in and out of rapport periodically during the course of a conversation, however, we should continue to monitor the interpersonal connection. Rapport occasionally needs to be reestablished during an interaction.

Communication is simply a process of sending and receiving feedback for the purpose of understanding. The *skill* and *will* to communicate effectively are choices.

The chances are good that you already know how to communicate more effectively than you actually practice. Choose to use your communication skills more effectively at work and at home and experience greater relationship fulfillment.

AWARENESS CHECKS

- How well are you choosing to communicate at home and at work? Do you note a difference between those two environments?

- To what extent do you demonstrate safety when receiving feedback?

- Where might you be holding back on your courage to communicate?

- What communication skills might be enhanced in your personal and professional settings?

- What is the learning?

"Truth is always the strongest argument."

Sophocles

17

Feedback Is a Gift:
"TELL ME MORE!"

**"Seek first to understand,
then to be understood."**

Stephen R. Covey

A department director client of mine in a large organization said, "I used to get a lot of negative feedback about my department. I don't get that feedback anymore—things must be going better." A dangerous assumption! Having just interviewed all of his key leaders, I had acquired another perspective. Because of his poor working relationships, his associates were all considering quitting at the same time. And he thought things were going well!

How could such a condition have developed without the department director knowing? Basically, he taught the department leaders *not* to give him feedback. Some months previously, he had called a meeting of key leaders to identify and resolve departmental issues "once and for all." When he asked for feedback, one brave individual shared several negative comments about departmental operations. The department director became outraged, pointed his finger at the individual, and said, "You! Out in the hall!" In front of her peers, this person was literally ordered by the department head to stand in the hall.

For some strange reason, feedback to the department director stopped at that point! Although "parking lot" conversations buzzed, no one was willing to talk to him. Communication with the boss had clearly become unsafe, and he was effectively cut out of the direct communication flow.

Sometimes individuals insulate themselves from feedback, creating a closed, low-trust environment. Parking lot meetings occur as communication channels erode and people look for other outlets to share what they are thinking, feeling, and wanting.

Anyone with an IQ of 2 or less knows that ordering an associate out into the hall for giving feedback is a poor action, yet in subtle ways, we sometimes "order" others to "stand out in the hall" by not listening or paying attention to feedback.

In my first marriage, I may as well have ordered my wife to "stand out in the hall." Let me explain. I am a good problem solver. When issues arose, my problem-solving skills kicked into high gear. On occasion, she wanted to vent her feelings. Not problem solve, just vent. As soon as she started, my brain went to work. A problem to solve! Quick, solve the problem. "Now, what's your next problem?" While not quite that crass, my behaviors over a long period of time demonstrated a poor ability to just listen and be with her as she sought to talk and connect. By making communication difficult and uncomfortable, I basically taught her to withhold and withdraw.

Consider the situation of someone who is angry and literally or figuratively yelling in your face! How might you react? Yell back (*attack* mode). What happens to the intensity of the other person's emotions when you yell back? They escalate and the

186

conflict situation intensifies. Another approach might be to say, "I don't have to put up with this stuff," then abruptly walk out of the room, slamming the door behind you (*avoidance* mode). What happens to the intensity of the other person's emotions now? They escalate again! Is the situation resolved by leaving? No. While neither approach works, both are commonly used conflict strategies. Both resistance forms ignore internal resources and contribute to the acceleration of conflict. Neither provides the safety to explore and discover.

Punch through your wall of resistance.

Another strategy tends to produce more favorable results. Be prepared, for this involves pausing and going *into* your resistance to learn from feedback. Imagine a wall of resistance between you and your critic. Instead of attacking or avoiding that wall, cut a doorway in your wall and walk through. Your greatest opportunity to learn and grow usually rests on the other side. Five steps are involved in punching through your areas of resistance when in conflict:

1. Pause. Not just a time intermission, pausing provides a conscious opportunity to maximize your inner resources through a head-heart connection. Awareness of internal resistance serves as a signal to pause for internal resourcing and elevation of consciousness. Use resistance as a resource.

2. "Tell me more." You've got to be kidding! *"Tell me more?"* Why should I listen under these circumstances? While the natural human response would be to verbally attack, shifting to this quiet, active listening mode creates a conscious presence. Role modeling safety in listening frequently becomes contagious. If you are experiencing resistance to this suggestion, perhaps a learning opportunity is close at hand!

187

3. Listen with every bone in your body. Often, rather than listening, waiting to talk and rearranging prejudices become our focal point. When we are waiting to talk, our mind focuses on preparing a rebuttal and justifying our position. That's not listening. "Seek first to understand, then to be understood," encourages author Stephen Covey (1989). Listening with the intent of understanding enables us to build rapport—even in stressful situations. Usually, we want to be understood before understanding others. So do they. With both of us seeking to be understood, active listening gives way to preparing a rebuttal and gaining the upper hand. Instead, seek first to understand the facts, as well as the other person's perception and interests. Empathetic listening assists in clarifying and resolving issues, developing rapport, and guiding relationship bridges.

4. Find a way to agree with your critic. Agree? Yes—with the other person's perceptions and with the facts of the situation. Remember the thirty-square exercise in Chapter 7? You might see sixteen squares while your critic sees twenty-five. The converse may also be true, yet you will never know unless you become quiet inside and listen. Encourage your critic to walk you through the way he or she experiences reality and look for the learning. Acknowledge the other person's perspective and feelings: "Now I have a better understanding of how you see this situation," or "Your perspective is important to me, and I understand how you feel," or "Yes, those facts are correct. Can I share another perspective?" Through active mutual listening, the two of you together are likely to discover the thirty squares—more than either observed alone.

5. Reward feedback—feedback is a gift. Rewarding feedback with a simple "thank you" also helps to build relationships and reinforce open communication. When an employee or boss gives you feedback you don't particularly appreciate, reward the feedback with: "Thank you for caring enough about me to share that sensitive feedback. While some of that was hard for me to hear, I will give it consideration and look for the learning. Please continue to talk directly with me on other issues." By doing this, you encourage others to continue coming back to you for caring straight talk rather than having indirect parking lot conversations with others about you.

Feedback is a gift. Whether we like, understand, or appreciate the feedback makes no difference. By encouraging feedback, we learn and grow. We connect with people. We learn more about our blind spots and create new choice points. We develop trust and rapport with others and learn to make a difference. Encouraging and rewarding clear, open feedback from others provides ideas for improving our personal and professional effectiveness.

What if you were to practice these five steps when receiving tough feedback? What is likely to happen to the intensity of the other person's emotions? In most cases, emotional intensity declines. Understanding increases. Rapport builds. And people connect.

In my field, I am frequently involved with conflict-resolution work between individuals in organizations. I continue to be amazed at the power of the pausing process in enhancing understanding and building bridges. The best results occur when individuals are willing to pause and explore the areas typically resisted. Providing emotional safety for others to give feedback desensitizes the situation and models open behaviors. Active listening becomes contagious.

Periodically asking for feedback and listening for understanding assists in building safety in both your work and home environments. When relationship tension arises, active listening becomes even more important. By seeking to understand both the content and feelings of others, you create an opportunity to connect.

Is it safe for me to be me when I am with you?

"Is it safe for me to be me when I am with you?" Does the listener provide a safe environment in which I can share what I am thinking, feeling, and wanting? I need to have confidence that giving feedback to the listener will not come back to haunt me now or later. When I feel safe, I can be my Real Me in communicating with you.

By criticizing others' comments, becoming defensive, or basically getting back at them in some way, we teach people not to give us feedback. How might you be blocking feedback from others?

AWARENESS CHECKS

Do I block feedback by:

- Criticizing others' comments?
- Becoming defensive, reacting emotionally?
- Waiting to talk rather than listening?
- Being "too busy"?
- Preparing my rebuttal: "Yes, but . . ."?
- Keeping score—looking to get even?
- Interrupting, talking?
- Finding flaws in others' ideas and perceptions?
- Switching to my own agenda?
- Explaining, intellectualizing?
- Focusing on personalities, missing issues?
- Initiating premature closure?
- Locking onto my position?
- Rolling eyes, sighing, tapping fingers?
- Checking out—glazed eyes?
- Leaving when things get sensitive?
- Placing conditions on my availability to talk?

If we are really good at blocking feedback, we will experience major wake-up calls from time to time. By failing to create a safe environment for regular, timely feedback, we find that our enormous blind spots show up periodically as surprises "out of the blue." "Without warning," our employees walk off the job, our boss gives us a poor performance evaluation, our spouse develops an interest in someone else, our children have a brush with the law. And we wonder: "Where did this come from? Does this have something to do with me?"

Life provides very few real surprises. In most cases, advance information seeks to penetrate our communication filters. However, we teach others to withhold information when we do not actively listen or are unavailable. The costs of blocking feedback can be high.

We are always teaching others how to behave toward us.

Do you receive enough recognition and appreciation from the people who are important to you? If not, the chances are that you don't *give* enough feedback to satisfy their needs. Usually what you get back merely mirrors what you give to others. Simply put, if you are not receiving enough positive feedback, you are usually not giving enough positive feedback. You also can teach others *not* to acknowledge you and give positive feedback. Consider when someone last gave you a genuine compliment. Did you accept it with a simple "thank you"? Or did you deflect, discourage, or diminish the positive feedback?

When I complimented a woman on her dress, she responded, "This dress? This is going in the Goodwill bag as soon as I get home!" What did she teach me? That I have poor taste, and that she feels too uncomfortable with the feedback to receive it. On another occasion, someone complimented me on my tie. I quickly responded, "I like your tie, too!" When I looked **191** up, I discovered that he was not wearing a tie! Have you given a genuine compliment to someone only to have it diminished with a quick countercompliment? To encourage the continued flow of positive feedback, learn to say "thank you." End of discussion. Beginning of new experience in receiving more positive feedback.

Be inconsistent in giving feedback!

Many of us have been taught to be consistent when we give feedback by starting with the positive feedback and following with the downside or negative feedback. If we are consistent with this pattern over an extended period, we train people to prepare for negative feedback as soon as we begin with a compliment. They may even become resentful of the positive feedback, feeling that we are using an introductory compliment merely as a vehicle to get to the "real stuff." The listener braces for anticipated negative feedback as soon as we start with what appears superficially to be a positive statement.

Instead of becoming locked into a positive-to-negative feedback pattern, be inconsistent! At times, give only positive feedback—provided, of course, that the feedback is genuine. On other occasions, give only downside or negative feedback to the same individual. However, remember to separate the person from the problem and honor the individual; for example: "I genuinely respect and value you as a person and look forward to a long-term working relationship. At the same time, I am concerned about broken agreements regarding your three overdue reports. I want to be able to count on your completion dates to be accurate." Other situations may require linking positive and negative feedback together. If we are inconsistent in the *patterns* of giving feedback, yet consistently honest, listeners will grant us higher credibility and pay more attention to our feedback. And our straight talk will influence them with integrity.

Providing safety creates a foundation for building understanding. In most cases, we want to be understood first. So does the other person. We both lose as each of us increases our speaker volume while shutting off our receivers.

A number of my management clients have periodic feedback sessions with their associates for the purpose of enhancing their own leadership effectiveness. What better source of information exists than the very people we lead? In personal relationships as well, periodic feedback sessions related to reinforcing what is going well and candidly exploring opportunities for improvement can make a positive difference. This process can build even stronger relationship loyalty and commitment while functioning as a positive model of open, caring communication.

On a scale of 0 to 10, with 10 being highest, how safe do you make it for others to give you feedback at home? At work? What differences, if any, exist between the two environments? Which is safest and why? I often find that people create a safer environment at work than at home. They may exercise great care to communicate well in their professional environment, yet allow themselves to become sloppy in communicating with those with whom they are closest. Then they get a wake-up call and wonder why.

Quality communication requires exercising courage when giving feedback and providing safety when receiving feedback. Make it easy for others to provide you with feedback. Ask for it regularly and reward it. Be a resource of feedback safety. Since growth and development require quality feedback, create a climate that encourages it. Feedback is a gift.

18

Influential Listening:
THE POWER OF SILENCE

"Listening is a magnetic and strange thing, a creative force. The friends who listen to us are the ones we move toward, and we want to sit in their radius. When we are listened to, it creates us, makes us unfold and expand."

Karl Menninger

IN THE WEEKS PRECEDING the 1991 Persian Gulf War with Iraq, James Baker, U.S. secretary of state, and Tariq Aziz, Iraqi foreign minister, met to explore a peaceful solution. Prior to that meeting, Secretary Baker announced that he was going to tell the foreign minister "to his face" that there would be "no negotiations." Iraq must make an immediate and unconditional withdrawal from Kuwait or experience the consequences of the Allied military forces. Foreign

Minister Aziz also assumed a fixed position and announced that he would tell Secretary Baker that withdrawal of military forces would occur only if the Palestinian-Israeli issue were discussed. Neither was willing to listen to the other.

During the final six-hour meeting preceding the war, both sides functioned as loudspeakers blaring at one another. No pausing. No saying, "Tell me more." No listening. No seeking first to understand. Each man defended and advocated his own position. Each waited to talk. Neither one influenced or was influenced. Yes, the Middle East issue is complicated, and the atrocities imposed on the world by the leaders of Iraq could not be tolerated. Yet these critical diplomatic moments required quality listening skills and a commitment to understand. (As previously noted, our values are not tested when things are going well; the test occurs when things are *not* going well.)

At the conclusion of this meeting intended to prevent war, both Mr. Baker and Mr. Aziz independently addressed the international press corps to share their version of what occurred in this most critical session. Both charged that the other did not listen! And we went to war. Immediately following the war, international attention focused on (guess what!) the Palestinian-Israeli issue. Now people were willing to listen. How many times in our personal relationships have we "gone to war" rather than seeking understanding, and then ended up dealing with the original issue only after we paid the price of "war"? Wake-up calls. Choice points.

Active listening is one of the highest forms of giving.

Active listening, being fully present for another person, is regarded as one of the highest forms of giving. Stephen Covey (1989) encourages listening with the *intent* to understand. Through our choice to actively listen, we enhance our awareness, generate more options, and provide a foundation on which we can build relationships. Empathetic listening opens up the channels of communication and demonstrates that we value the other person. Functioning with conscious silence expands awareness. Listening provides options to resolve our differences.

For a moment, consider those people who have actively listened to you in the past. They were fully present and chose to eliminate distractions. They not only listened to your content; they understood your feelings. They accepted you and observed rather than judged you. You felt important and valued, you ended up valuing their opinion, and you continued to seek them out. Active listeners probably have been a significant influence in your life. Effective listeners become highly influential. Influential listening. What a paradox.

WHILE I CONDUCTED a three-day communication seminar for executives, an associate joined me as I functioned as her "master teacher" in the field of organization development. One of the class participants demonstrated particularly poor communication skills throughout the session. He frequently interrupted, attempted to take us off course, and made many inappropriate comments. My patience wore thin. When the three-day seminar ended, the others left, but he stayed. As my associate and I gathered our materials together, he continued to badger me with numerous questions and inappropriate remarks. I felt my face redden and my ears become warmer. I had reached my limit with this guy.

Observing my angered state, my "student teacher" slowly walked over and joined us. Observing his attempts to communicate with me, she said to him, "You are really hurting, aren't you?" He burst into tears! I had focused on his "inappropriate content" and missed his deep hurt. He was so unskilled in interpersonal communication that people stopped listening and withdrew whenever he spoke. As they began to pull away, he intensified his unskilled efforts at communication.

His pattern typified a communication stuck state, yet he was working on his stuff—even by taking my communication seminar. And I wasn't listening with the intent of understanding. **197**

My "student teacher" became my master teacher at that moment. Through influential listening, she initiated a breakthrough with this client. What a powerful learning for me. She gave me a gift for which I am ever grateful and remains my teacher for empathetic listening.

Are we listening—or waiting to talk?

Instead of actively listening, we engage in the internal dialogue of waiting to talk, preparing our rebuttal, or rearranging our prejudices. These dysfunctional practices reflect *simulated,* not active, listening. Evidence of ignoring the speaker's input occurs when we interrupt with a "Yes, but . . ." statement. Someone referred to the word "but" as the "great eraser." Everything in front of the word "but" is erased, while our real message follows. "I agree with you, *but* . . . ," "I love you, *but* . . . ," "I think you are doing a great job, *but* . . ." A more congruent outcome results from using the word "and" in place of "but." "I agree, *and* another perspective worth considering is . . . ," "I love you, *and* parts of our relationship can function even better," "I am pleased with the quality of your work, *and* several opportunities exist to get even better results."

Being understood and accepted are fundamental human needs. Active listening provides one of the most effective mechanisms for fulfilling this need. By seeking first to understand, we behaviorally communicate respect to the speaker. Listening with intent creates a reciprocal climate that also enables us to be understood in the process—after we have consciously listened to the content and feelings of the other person's message. However, if we are "listening" just for the purpose of later being understood, no connection occurs and relationship tension increases. A significant difference exists between listening and waiting to talk.

Identifying and meeting interests enhances influential listening. In their book *Getting to Yes* (1983), authors Roger Fisher and William Ury emphasize the importance of transcending positions while seeking mutual interests as a win-win negotiation practice. Active listening is a strategic process to bring divergent interests together.

THE MIDDLE EAST PROVIDES A COMPELLING example of influencing through active listening. During the Six-Day War in 1967, Israel "acquired" a large chunk of land from Egypt. For a decade, significant tension existed between the two countries as each demanded ownership of the land. Both countries locked into an impasse position. Israel would not give up that land, and Egypt would not permit Israel to occupy it.

In the late 1970s, President Jimmy Carter brought the leaders of Israel and Egypt together at Camp David to work out a lasting solution. Progress was slow and difficult, and the leaders remained fixed in their positions. An exploration of the *interests* behind their positions, however, began to generate new levels of awareness and new choices. *Why* did Israel want the land—what was its interest? Safety and security. As long as enemy troops and equipment were at Israel's border, its security was in jeopardy. *Why* did Egypt want the land—what was its interest? Saving face and sovereignty. The land belonged to Egypt, and it had been taken away in the spoils of war.

When they focused on and listened to the *interests* behind their respective positions, both sides influenced one another. On the surface, the Camp David accord appeared to be a compromise. A compromise, however, would have resulted in merely dividing the land in half, and moving the border would only have prolonged the hostilities.

Instead, a collaborative solution that met the countries' mutual interests was achieved. The land was returned to Egypt, and that country's flag flies over the territory. Egypt fully attained its *interest* of saving face and sovereignty. On the other hand, no military forces and no military weapons are located in the disputed land. Israel fully achieved its *interest* of safety and security. What amazing results creative minds can accomplish when people choose to listen! This was a powerful demonstration of influential listening.

GUIDELINES FOR INFLUENTIAL LISTENING

1. Listen with a head-heart connection—pause.
2. Listen with the intent of understanding.
3. Listen for the message and the message behind the message.
4. Listen for both content and feelings.
5. Listen with your eyes—your hearing will be improved.
6. Listen for others' interests, not just their position.
7. Listen for what they are saying and *not* saying.
8. Listen with empathy and acceptance.
9. Listen for the areas where they are afraid and hurt.
10. Listen as you would like to be listened to.

Bring to mind a difficult interpersonal situation in which you and another individual have a markedly different perspective or position. Look behind the other person's position for a possible core interest. What does she want? A *position* often masks a person's real *interest.* For example, someone might claim to want a "deep, loving relationship," while his real interest may be protection from getting hurt. An individual at work may seek to relocate her office to one having a window; her real interest might be to enhance her status and self-worth and to feel more appreciated.

WHEN I WORKED IN HOSPITAL ADMINISTRATION, a laboratory technologist told me of her desire to form a union of clinical professionals. Her desire to form the union did not come from problems with the administration. Instead, she expressed the concern that clinical professionals might be drafted into an inappropriate trade union that was currently organizing within the hospital. I was in an awkward position. On one hand, I needed to be careful not to interfere with the employees' right to organize. On the other hand, I preferred to have the ability to work and communicate directly with employees rather than through a third-party union. An opportunity for influential listening presented itself.

I asked the technologist to describe the advantages and disadvantages of unionization and what she wanted to accomplish. Rapport developed as I listened without guiding her one way or the other. In the process, I learned that she was bored with her job and had untapped leadership capabilities. Active participation in forming a union enabled her to gain new experiences while applying her leadership talents.

At the same time, a need existed within the hospital to form an educational program that would link various health-care professionals together in an effort to better serve patients. We also needed to expand our community health education program as part of our community service responsibilities. During the course of my conversation with the technologist, I shared these needs. Her eyes sparkled as she leaned forward to further explore these important yet undeveloped programs. Her interest peaked!

Through active listening, I learned the essence of her interests. While her "position" focused on forming a union, her real interest was to make a positive contribution while developing and applying her untapped leadership potential. Her talents matched the hospital's needs—a win-win outcome. She became the focal point in developing a comprehensive health education program called "Interface." Highly successful results further stimulated her to pursue a career in hospital administration. Some years later, I had the privilege of helping her gain acceptance into a graduate course in health-care administration.

Listen with intent.

A skeptic of influential listening might conclude that the process is manipulative. *Intent* becomes the **201** guiding force. Genie Laborde, author of *Influencing with Integrity* (1984), concludes that manipulation is "achieving your own outcome at the expense of or even without regard for the other party." Achieving *mutual* interests or outcomes, on the other hand, influences with a spirit of partnership and accountability. You have the responsibility of listening with awareness and functioning with integrity as you influence the thought processes of others. Yes, this process can be abused. Intent is a choice, and you are clearly in charge of that choice.

Communication barriers can be transcended by consciously applying the ten guidelines for influential listening. Empathetic listening honors the speaker as an individual and positions him or her to be more receptive while building relationship trust.

Listen with a head-heart connection to the speaker's messages. Listen for both content and feelings. Listen with the intent of understanding. Active listening enhances your ability to understand and be understood—and to make a positive difference.

Part 4

MAKING A
DIFFERENCE

Differences Are Resources:

VALUING OUR UNIQUENESS

"You must pay for conformity."

Ralph Waldo Emerson

What if everyone in the world were just like you? As neat as you are, the world simply wouldn't work. Can you imagine how boring the world would be if everyone thought and behaved like you? We need differences. They are resources, not deficiencies. Variations contribute to life's richness and stimulate learning, enabling us to develop new insights and self-awareness. Distinctions contribute to creativity, stimulate ideas, and challenge us to be our best. Consider this: When two businesspeople always agree, one of them is unnecessary.

Each of us has a unique set of talents that almost magically contributes to the perfection of the universe. Sometimes we focus on these differences as flaws and miss their value. What if we looked past the differences and discovered their benefits?

Seek unity, not uniformity.

Suppose we are on an organizational team that has a vacant position. In seeking to fill this position, we often look for an individual who agrees with our philosophy, yet complements us through his or her unique experience and training. We look for a fresh perspective, new ideas, new blood.

After our search, we find the "perfect" combination of similarities and differences within a single candidate. This person has a brilliant history of contributing at her past place of employment and is credited with generating numerous useful ideas. With enthusiasm, we bring her on board. The candidate shares our excitement. Soon, she taps into her differences by sharing a number of ideas that might lead to enhanced effectiveness.

How do you suppose these ideas are received? You've got it—resistance! We begin hearing such things as, "We tried that before, and it didn't work." "In this organization, we do it this way." "The boss will never buy it." "You haven't been here long enough to understand." "It's not in the budget." We begin chipping off the new person's "corners." The very reasons we hired her related to her differences, or corners, and we immediately dishonor those unique elements. In the process, we make her just like the rest of us! We create another one of us.

What do employees learn? To hold back, to stifle ideas. They quickly learn that differences are neither supported nor appreciated. Associates learn the risks of sharing ideas and eventually choose to conform. What results do we experience, organizationally and individually? Organizationally, we lose the benefits of people's differences. We seal off the passage to their

206

DIFFERENCES AS "DEFICIENCIES"

Phase One:
We have a need.

Phase Two:
We fill the void with someone who agrees with our philosophy, yet offers differences.

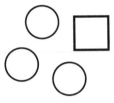

Phase Three:
We chip away at the person's corners by finding fault with his or her differences.

creativity. We deny access to the very qualities that enable them to be effective and to experience personal fulfillment. And a part of them dies in the process. What a demotivating and dishonoring experience.

Would you believe that we do the same thing in our personal relationships as well? Often, individual differences become the force that attracts two people. For example, John is attracted to Linda's sensitivity. After being in a long-term relationship with Linda, however, John becomes distracted by that same sensitivity and says, "You are so sensitive. No matter what

207

I say or do, your feelings get hurt. Why can't you be stronger?" In another example, Christina is favorably impressed by Richard's particular sense of justice and strong value system. Later, she becomes distracted by his inflexibility and narrow perspective and says, "You are so locked in. You make everything into a big moral issue. Why can't you loosen up?" We end up asking ourselves, "Why can't they be more like *me?*" Notice how we round off corners when we treat differences as deficiencies.

"The surest way to corrupt a youth is to instruct him to hold in higher esteem those who think alike than those who think differently."

Friedrich Nietzsche

I AM REMINDED OF A STORY ABOUT a six-year-old boy who, for half of his life, had been looking forward to going to school. He could finally join his older brother and sister in this important life step. With an open mind and excited about being in school, he sat in the front row—eager to discover and learn. The first-grade teacher, with a smile on her face, said, "Today, children, we are going to have an art lesson." The boy's creativity kicked into high gear! He thought to himself, "I could make things out of clay. I could draw things. I could do finger painting. I could build things out of blocks. I could . . ." Just then, his creative process was interrupted by the teacher, who said, "Today, children, we are going to have a drawing lesson." Again his creative mind took over. He thought, "I could draw ships, airplanes, mountains, trees." The teacher then said, "Today, children, we are going to learn how to draw flowers." The boy, now beginning to learn that what the teacher wanted was perhaps more important than his interests, still remained in a creative mode. He thought, "I could draw sunflowers, roses, dandelions." Then the teacher said, "Today, children, we are going to learn to draw medium-sized red tulips."

Only one year later, in the second grade, the boy has already learned to contain his creativity. On the first day of the second grade, a choice point confronted him with a brand-new teacher and a brand-new classroom. The new teacher said to the students, "Today, children, we are going to have an art lesson—and you can do anything you want to do!" The boy thought for a moment—and drew a medium-sized red tulip.

"One man with courage makes a majority."

Andrew Jackson

We begin life as a giant question mark. Everything is brand-new and open for exploration and discovery. We are diamonds in the rough. By the time we complete high school, we are a giant period. We know how it is. We know the answers we are supposed to know. Our creativity has been channeled. Our edges have been smoothed. We have been acculturated.

"Education for creative people begins when they leave school," reported Gay Hendricks at a seminar. I can personally relate to that in my own experience. In my senior year in high school, the guidance counselor called me into her office in response to my application for a scholarship. She said, "If I have anything to do with it, you will not get this scholarship." She further suggested that I change my course of study and explained that I would never make it through higher education, so the college preparatory courses I was enrolled in were just a waste of time. Instead, she wanted me to change my program to vocational studies such as auto mechanics or carpentry.

At the time, my grade-point average was a solid "B+," I was taking advanced placement academic classes, and I was serving as student body president. Somehow her assessment did not fit, and I was gutsy enough even at the time to ignore her counsel. From other sources, I knew her to have strong prejudices about **209**

African-American students. Since I was actively involved in building interracial relationships, my activities ran counter to her belief system. She saw an opportunity to chip off my corners and chose to act. In that situation, I simply did not allow her to round my corners. I did go on to college—supported partially by the scholarship she tried to withhold from me.

Two dimensions are essential in both organizational and individual relationships in order for us to work and live together harmoniously: (1) honor the differences (respect the "wild duck" element) and (2) agree on a larger mission, purpose, or direction that we can passionately pursue together (fly in formation). Honoring differences empowers us all to be the very best we can be and encourages us to use and develop our "corners." Aware empowerment provides latitude for us to use our good stuff! Instead of chipping off the corners, we celebrate differences and uniqueness. We need the *wild ducks* and we need the wild ducks to *fly in formation*. The combination of these two elements represents the foundation of high-quality personal and organizational relationships. Seek unity, not uniformity.

What if you committed to creating giants of others?

ALFRED SLOAN, THE CELEBRATED FORMER PRESI-DENT of General Motors, was struggling with a major policy issue. He called in his chief advisers to gain the advantage of their experience and counsel. At the close of their deliberations, he asked each executive around the conference table where he or she stood on the issue. Solid support. In fact, a unanimous decision had been reached by the top executives. Most presidents would have been delighted by a majority vote, let alone unanimous support. Not Alfred Sloan.

At that point, he delivered a message to his advisers, which I paraphrase here: "Because we are in unanimous agreement on this critical issue, I am tabling the decision. We cannot afford to

DIFFERENCES ARE RESOURCES

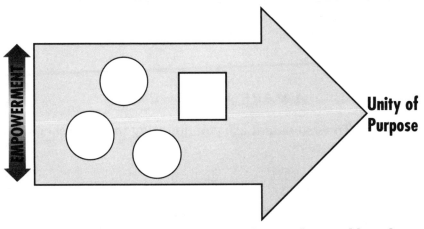

Our Relationship Challenge Is to Empower the "Wild Ducks" to Fly in Formation!

- "Empowerment" provides latitude for the "wild ducks" to use their talents—and their corners.

- "Flying in formation" encourages unity of purpose, not uniformity.

have each of us of the same opinion. I am paying for your judgment, not for your agreement." He tabled the decision because he believed that if everyone thinks the same way, not much thinking is going on. Some weeks later, they revisited the issue—and developed a more effective solution than the one they had unanimously supported. What did Sloan teach them? That it is safe to disagree. That differences are valued and welcomed. That different perspectives enrich the decision-making process. That differences are resources.

Honoring and empowering differences within a context of philosophical agreement creates giants of yourself and others. I am not advocating that you "get your ducks in a row." That process creates midgets of others. A more challenging and

211

fulfilling practice creates a situation where "wild ducks fly in formation." That commitment creates giants of others. Honoring the spirit of unity, not uniformity, brings out the uniqueness in others while serving a shared purpose.

AWARENESS CHECKS

◖ To what extent are you honoring the differences of others:

- At work?
- At home?

◖ How might you be "chipping off the corners" of your:

- Co-workers?
- Children?
- Partner?

◖ To what extent are you chipping off your own corners?

◖ What is the learning here?

Relationship Gaps and Bridges:
MAKING IT WORK

"There is no way to happiness. Happiness is the way."

Wayne Dyer

Living at the same address does not necessarily result in emotional closeness. Sometimes the closer we are to people, the more distant the relationship! Unfulfilled expectations, both at home and at work, often become the source of tension that eventually erodes the very fabric of quality relationships. We frequently lack clarity about our wants, needs, and expectations, yet become frustrated and angry when these unspoken relationship requirements are not met. After all, if he really loved me, he would *know* what I want and need. We expect the other person to read our mind, while subtly punishing that person by withholding, withdrawing, and perhaps even attacking when our needs are not met. Relationship gaps widen and wake-up calls emerge.

"Love is a decision and a commitment."

John Powell

Love is a decision? Yes, love is a conscious choice not only to be with your partner, but to *be* with your partner. To be fully present. To share your thoughts, feelings, and wants. To share your joy, fears, frustrations, successes, shortcomings, and dreams. To support and be supported. To contribute to your partner's growth and development. And to honor his or her individuality. A tall order? Yes. Yet the *choice* creates closeness; sleepwalking through your relationship creates distance.

AWARENESS CHECKS

- On a scale of 0 to 10, how would you rate your most important relationship?
- What specifically would it take to create a 10?
- What can you do differently and what can your partner do differently to make a positive difference?
- What are you *willing* to do differently to build relationship bridges?
- What is the learning?

Examine your most important relationship. On a scale of 0 to 10, with 10 being highest, what number would you assign the current quality of your relationship? A 5, a 9, a 2? I encourage you to conscientiously apply Relationship Enhancement Exercise 1 to assist in making a positive difference in your relationship. Working together in the spirit of partnership, you can take specific steps toward creating a 10!

Notice the "Strength-Stretch" language in the following exercise. When you interact with your partner, careful attention should be given to both acknowledging *strengths* or "well dones" and working through the *stretches* or opportunities for improvement. Issues requiring attention should be explored with openness and sensitivity. In a spirit of partnership, address the issues while building relationship bridges. Such caring straight talk encourages your partner to join rather than resist in the problem-solving process. *How* you communicate is as important as *what* is communicated.

The follow-up to the relationship enhancement process assists in bringing about long-term, positive results. By setting a follow-up date to take place as soon as the first exchange has been completed, both partners can use "creative stress" to honor both the letter and spirit of their commitments. The follow-up exchange has two purposes: (1) celebrating positive results, even if they are relatively small, and (2) consciously self-correcting to stay on track. Make the follow-up celebration fun by rewarding yourselves with something you both would enjoy: dinner at that special restaurant, a weekend holiday without the kids, a long walk—whatever works best for you.

Are you holding back in your relationship?

Love, trust, and acceptance are either conditional or unconditional. The conditions themselves create distance between us and our partner. Often, we set up a series of hoops for our partner to jump through to demonstrate commitment and to satisfy our needs. If, by chance, our partner successfully jumps through all those hoops, do we fully and finally accept him or her? No! We tend to add more hoops! (Not *you*, of course. People who are less aware than you tend to do this.)

215

Relationship Enhancement Exercise 1

Step 1: Each partner first works alone to identify strengths and stretches.
Step 2: In an atmosphere of caring straight talk, each partner then shares his or her list—seeking first to understand, then to be understood.
Step 3: Commitments are made with a clear agreement to follow up on a specified date.

Strengths: I appreciate the following about our relationship:

_____

_____

_____

_____

Stretches: To bring our relationship to a 10, I want *more* of the following:

_____

_____

_____

_____

Stretches: To bring our relationship to a 10, I want *less* of the following:

_____

_____

_____

_____

Commitments: To enhance our relationship, I commit to the following:

_____

_____

_____

_____

Follow-up: On _____(date)_____, we will set aside time to:

1. Celebrate our "stretch" successes
2. Self-correct, where appropriate, to make a positive difference

216

Relationships can be viewed from two perspectives: (1) What can I get *from* this relationship and (2) what can I give *to* this relationship. If our primary interest is to acquire fulfillment *from* the relationship, we will ultimately use up the resources of our partner. The quality of the relationship is not measured by what we are able to take from the interaction, but by what we bring to it.

Often we will hear people say, "Don't take me for granted!" Or we might hear, "Don't take my love for granted!" What is the message behind the message? Do these words suggest conditions that must be met before such people will fully commit themselves? Or do the words indirectly imply unfulfilled expectations? Whichever is the case, pausing *right now* for mutual understanding is essential. Do not let this one go by without thorough exploration.

According to John Powell, author of *Unconditional Love* (1978), loving unconditionally behaviorally says, "Take me and take my love for granted." Where and in what circumstances do you withhold love? What if you loved unconditionally? Through this conscious commitment, you create a spirit of connectedness that results in a meaningful relationship. While it takes two to make a relationship, it takes only one to change it. You are in charge of shaping your relationship. What do you want to create? What is a 10 for you? To what extent are you willing to commit to doing whatever it takes to build a 10?

While a different dimension, quality relations in a work environment are equally important. A bank president recently shared his loan approval philosophy with me:

> When considering a loan application from two business partners, of course I thoroughly review their financial reports and carefully apply the standard financial tests. The bottom line for me, however, is "Do they love each other?" Even if the numbers are positive, if they don't love each other, the loan is likely to be a high risk. If they do love each other, their commitment to one another will carry them through significant business adversity. Their loving each other reduces my financial risk and creates a foundation for a safe, long-term investment in their business venture.

217

When a bank president's "bottom-line" for a loan approval is the quality of the business relationship, an entirely new significance is placed on this intangible dimension. We cannot ignore relationship issues in our work environment.

Unpack your bags!

I read about an attorney who had prepared well over a hundred premarital agreements for couples to protect their respective assets in the event that their pending marriage did not work out. To many, this appears to be a prudent, businesslike practice that would avoid future problems if and when a separation occurred. While this makes sense on the surface, let's look at what this practice communicates. You guessed it: conditional love. Strings. Escape routes that may actually encourage limited-commitment thinking.

The attorney's professional experience with premarital agreements was tragically interesting: Every marriage ultimately ended in divorce! No exceptions. When people enter a relationship with their bags packed—just in case—they may consciously or unconsciously create a limited, conditional mindset that becomes a self-fulfilling prophecy. The lesson? Unpack your bags! The real test of our values is not when things are going well; the real test is when things are *not* going well. When relationship difficulties occur, and that will happen, having your emotional bags unpacked communicates a clear commitment to work things through, provides a fertile environment to solve problems, and builds relationships. This "count on me to be there for you" attitude in itself takes the pressure off and enables both individuals to focus on the issues rather than be frozen by fear and threats.

Is it safe for me to be me when I am with you? Quality relating provides safety for me to openly share with you what I am thinking, feeling, and wanting. No reservations, no judgment.

218 Just accepting who I am and honoring where I am at this point in my development. Working through the relationship enhancement exercises in this chapter with an advance commitment to providing emotional safety will enable partners to deal effectively with the issues while simultaneously building the spirit of partnership—at home and at work.

While it takes two to make a relationship, it takes only one to change it.

Building positive relationships requires periodic "pauses" for self-assessment and exploration of how our ever-changing interactions can be enhanced. I have introduced literally thousands of executives to the partnership coaching process shown in Relationship Enhancement Exercise 2 with unusually consistent, positive results. In a corporate team development seminar, I ask individuals to identify others with whom they would like to have an even better working relationship. The executives then pair up and work through the exercise. For many, this is a major stretch. In a caring environment of straight talk, however, the vast majority create better understanding while growing even closer to one another. A similar, favorable result occurs when I work with couples in a personal setting.

Step 1 of this exercise reinforces your partner's strengths and honors his or her differences. Genuine acknowledgment of your partner's gifts and talents sets a positive climate while building rapport as the straight-talk exchange process begins.

Step 2 is a self-examination of what "I" do that gets in the way of the relationship, whether personal or professional. This approach encourages self-awareness and accountability while defusing sensitive issues. Items listed might include withholding caring, support, or feelings; not being "present"; unwillingness to move off my position; being judgmental; not listening; seeking to meet my needs at your expense; not meeting financial responsibilities; escaping accountability; or having "parking

Relationship Enhancement Exercise 2

Partnership Coaching

Seated and facing his or her partner, each person talks through Step 1. Messages are sent and received both ways for each step before the partners advance to the next step. (Stick to the steps, as they will assist you in working through important issues while building a spirit of partnership.)

Step 1. What I appreciate about you is . . .

_____

_____

Step 2. What I do that gets in the way of our (working) relationship is . . .

_____

_____

Step 3. I would like you to:

    a. Do more of or start doing . . .

_____

_____

    b. Do less of or stop doing . . .

_____

_____

Step 4. I commit to the following:

    a. Do more of or start doing . . .

_____

_____

    b. Do less of or stop doing . . .

_____

_____

Step 5. What else I appreciate about you is . . .

_____

_____

lot" meetings rather than communicating directly with you. A temptation frequently exists to focus on what the *other* person does that gets in the way; that approach results in a blame-victim exchange that increases relationship tension and widens the gap. With each partner instead responsibly focusing on his or her own stuff that creates relationship gaps, an open, safe environment results in accountable problem solving.

Step 3, "What I want from you," requires clarity and presence. Frequently individuals have difficulty expressing what they want from others. The challenge of fulfilling unexpressed expectations, therefore, becomes almost impossible for the other person. Give your partner or work associate a break. Express your interests, wants, and needs directly.

Step 4 focuses on what you are willing to do differently to enhance the quality of your personal or professional relationship. After sharing with your partner what you want more of and less of, and learning what your partner wants, you are now at a choice point. Step 4 sets the stage for a commitment in making a positive relationship difference. From an accountable perspective, you are now in a position to commit to action. In addition to a verbal commitment, write out your step 4 agreements and set a specific date, time, and place for a follow-up meeting. Reinforcement through follow-up becomes a powerful tool in making commitments stick.

Step 5 is an interesting experience. When partners communicate with caring and respect, they invariably discover additional qualities they genuinely appreciate about the other. Listening with the intent of understanding almost always closes relationship gaps and permits you to discover important qualities that were previously filtered out. Concluding the process on a positive note also encourages open communication when you next interact with your partner or professional associate.

Strengths-Stretches-Targets.

A third relationship enhancement exercise, called "S-S-T Relationship Coaching," introduces an impor- **221** tant element: *targets*. Targets refer to relationship goals or even purposes for being together. Having a shared vision or purpose is essential to building a quality relationship. Without clarity of direction and unity of relationship purpose, tension and confusion arise. This exercise assists in clarifying the *what* and *how* of expectations. *Targets* focus on what you want to create, *strengths* reinforce what is already going well, and *stretches* identify specifically how to accomplish your targets.

Targets may require more clarification. The following examples identify how this process could be used in both a personal and a professional environment:

1. Examples of *personal* relationship targets:

   - Honoring each other's individuality
   - Creating joy and relationship harmony
   - Building trust and open communication
   - Empowering one another to grow and develop
   - Creating an environment where each willingly commits
   - Creating both emotional and financial security
   - Building a strong, caring family environment

2. Examples of *professional* relationship targets:

   - Balancing productivity with human sensitivity
   - Building an empowered organization
   - Building trust and open communication
   - Fostering individual and organizational growth and development
   - Balancing individual and organizational needs
   - Creating a spirit of partnership
   - Delighting customers through quality products and services

Relationship Enhancement Exercise 3

S-S-T Relationship Coaching
(Strengths-Stretches-Targets)

Step 1: Each partner first works alone to identify relationship expectations specifically related to targets, strengths, and stretches. Targets focus on the goals, strengths reinforce what is already going well, and stretches identify specifically how to accomplish the targets.

Step 2: In an atmosphere of caring straight talk, each partner then shares his or her list—seeking first to understand, then to be understood.

Step 3: Commitments are made with a clear agreement to follow up on a specified date.

Targets: In the spirit of partnership, I would like to create with you the following relationship goals:

_____

_____

_____

Strengths: I appreciate the following about our relationship:

_____

_____

_____

Stretches: To enhance our relationship, I want *more* of the following:

_____

_____

_____

Stretches: To enhance our relationship, I want *less* of the following:

_____

_____

_____

Follow-up: On _____(date)_____ **, we will set aside time to:**

1. Celebrate our "stretch" successes

2. Self-correct, where appropriate, to make a positive difference

223

Mutually developed targets to which both people can fully and passionately commit are, in themselves, powerful tools in developing quality relationships. Meaningful relationship targets assist people in transcending their individual limits and draw upon their resources as a couple to make a positive difference. Take time individually and together to develop your relationship purposes and targets. The process then becomes even more valuable than the end product. The journey may be more important than the destination.

Closing gaps and building quality relationships requires individuals to be on "speaking terms" with one another at a high level. Talking straight in a caring way and listening for understanding are keys to fresh, healthy relationships. The strength-stretch-target methods described here provide a simple structure with which you can achieve major progress in making positive relationship differences. (My wife and I periodically apply this process to keep our relationship current, fulfilling, and joyful. And it works!) Be prepared for a wake-up call or two in the process. It is far better, however, to work through minor wake-up calls in this process than to experience a major surprise down the road. While it takes two to make a relationship, it takes only one to change it. What do you want in your relationship and what are you willing to do to create that result?

Closing the familiarity gap.

The closer we are to the people who are important in our lives, the sloppier we sometimes become in interpersonal communication and behavior. That is the "familiarity gap." Because these people are familiar to us (and because we are not awake), we inadvertently create relationship gaps, and relationship tension follows. For example, if a business associate spilled coffee on your couch, you might say, "Don't worry about it. It will come off easily." We just handle it. No big deal. But what happens when our spouse or children spill something on the couch? We attack! We are often toughest on those with whom we are the closest. While we don't want to be taken for granted, we may choose to take them for granted. We sleep-walk through important relationships. And what prices we pay!

HANS AND FRITA, A TRADITIONAL-STYLE COUPLE, have been married for forty years. Frita, reflecting on their relationship, finally developed the courage to say, "Hans, you never tell me that you love me anymore." Hans replied, "Frita, when we got married forty years ago, I told you that I loved you. If I change my mind, I'll let you know." The familiarity gap widens.

Check this out for yourself. With whom do you exercise greater care in communicating: your most valued customer or your spouse? How about your boss compared with your spouse? Care enough to communicate well—both at work and at home. Familiarity does generate certain advantages. We can be ourselves. We don't have to pretend or protect. We can just "let it all hang out." It's easy—sometimes too easy. The caring is taken for granted, and our behaviors eventually reflect the expectation that "you will be there for me even when I don't take very good care of you." Relationship tension increases ever so subtly. Our partner eventually gets sick and tired of not feeling special. Then we get a wake-up call.

Whenever we experience a gap between what we want in life and what we actually create, a wake-up call invariably awaits us. If we are not receiving enough recognition and appreciation, the chances are that we are not giving enough. If we are not receiving enough respect, or love, or support, or acceptance, it is very likely that we are holding back on these as well. What you get back in life usually mirrors what you put out. If you don't like what you are receiving, examine what you are giving. Usually we want more to come back to us than we are willing to put out, and we create a gap in the process. What gaps are you experiencing now and how do those gaps reflect your inner being? To what extent are you willing—unilaterally and unconditionally—to create relationship bridges?

225

A difference exists between a relationship and an entanglement, according to Gay and Kathlyn Hendricks in their book *Conscious Loving* (1990). In an entanglement, each partner places limits on the other. Both become less than whole. The result? One-half times one-half equals one-quarter! In a conscious, empowering relationship, one plus one equals two or more! The synergism of empowerment honors wholeness. Our conscious intent actively contributes to creating giants of others. What if we were to apply this principle unconditionally at work and at home? The resulting healing and aliveness would radiate throughout our life experience—and theirs. Imagine that.

Commitment:

UNPACK YOUR BAGS!

"Nothing of significance occurs until you commit."

Mary Manin Boggs

What you do has far greater significance than what you say. Your actions, as the saying goes, speak much more loudly than words. Words, however, are empowered through actions. When you commit and declare your commitment, things begin to happen. Commitment creates internal boldness and generates a sense of life in and of itself. It becomes an internal resource that enables you to accomplish what once was inconceivable.

Commitment links an important end state or future goal with present behavior. It reflects internal intentions that are lived out moment by moment. While it is a choice in itself, a commitment influences subsequent choices. These choices ultimately form the foundation of the quality of your journey as well as your destination. Commitments assist in determining what you say yes and no to in life. Part of your very identity is manifested through what you commit to—and the action you take.

> **"Without willingness to risk, there is no possibility."**
>
> John Hanley

Commitment requires the courage of convictions and a willingness to be vulnerable. Taking a stance necessitates putting yourself on the line—being "at stake," according to John Hanley (1989). You risk being wrong and surrender the opportunity to blend in with the masses. You are free right up to the moment of choice. Once you decide, that decision becomes your focus, and other options are intentionally dropped from consideration.

"Keeping your bags packed" in life and relationship situations signals your internal and external resources of your intention to—perhaps—move on. You communicate your ambiguity and unwillingness to be fully present in many subtle ways. Actions without commitment encourage others to both doubt your intentions and withhold their support. Lack of commitment is easily read and interpreted by others; it positions you to experience the very thing you often want to avoid. If you withhold yourself in a relationship for fear that this may not be "Mr. Right," the probability increases that you will experience a relationship crisis. If you hold back on the job because it isn't exactly what you expected, promotional opportunities and salary increases are unlikely to be manifested. Under these circumstances, you shut down and settle for less-than-optimal conditions. And a part of you dies.

If instead you unpack your bags and commit through words and actions to a defined result, things change. You experience

228

results and begin making a positive difference. You create more of what you want, regardless of external circumstances. And you experience life at a more fulfilling level.

A significant difference exists between commitment and interest. Consider a ham-and-egg breakfast: The pig is totally committed while the chicken has only a passing interest. The Vietnam War also demonstrated this concept. North Vietnam was totally committed to doing whatever it took to achieve its interests. All elements of society were absorbed in the war effort. The United States, on the other hand, considered it a "limited military action." Our sophisticated weapons and superior fighting force ultimately were no match for a Third World society committed to achieving its goals. North Vietnam's commitment eventually wore us down.

Majoring in minors is a costly way to do life.

As a SEMINAR PARTICIPANT several years ago, I was challenged with this question: What if your physician advised that you had only six to twelve months more to live? What, if anything, would you do differently in your relationships, your career, your family situation, your financial status, your spirituality? What commitments might you make? What actions would you implement?

Most of the seminar participants found that they would make significant changes in some element of their life. The late Michael Landon, after being diagnosed with terminal cancer, stated to the press: "Every little moment gets more important after something like this." What would become important to you under these circumstances? If you discover that significant changes are in order, that wake-up call may signal your need to reassess your life priorities and clarify what is important. Some of us use up an inordinate amount of our life experience on matters we later discover to be of little significance. Majoring in

229

minors is a costly way to do life. Awareness or understanding of the need to make changes is the first step. Taking action, however, becomes the essence of transformation. And that requires commitment.

Your life's work cannot be delegated to anyone else.

Making a difference starts with you. Your life's work cannot be delegated to anyone else. The following seven-step commitment process provides a tangible method of getting from where you are now to where you want to be, both personally and professionally. Bring to mind a major decision or commitment you are currently considering. You might be considering marriage, changing careers, dealing with substance abuse, going back to school, having another child, or purchasing a dream home. Let's walk through each step within the context of your pending decision.

Commitment Process: Seven Critical Steps

1. Clarify your values—what is important?
2. Identify your goals and interests—what do you want?
3. Create options to serve your values and goals.
4. Select a course of action consistent with your values and goals.
5. Declare a position "publicly."
6. Convert your commitment into action—unpack your bags!
7. Evaluate the results:
   - Celebrate successes
   - Take corrective action when appropriate

Step 1. Clarify your values—what is important?

A value-driven, principle-centered stance will generate far greater life fulfillment than merely reacting to current circumstances. Principle-centered commitments transcend time and conditions while assisting in clarifying what is important. When you are confronted with an issue, pause first and ask, "What principles or values will assist me in making a positive difference?" Making commitments within a context of principle provides clarity while serving as a guide in deciding both the *what* and the *how* related to the next steps.

Some years ago, I worked with an executive who found it difficult to take a stance under controversial conditions. "Keeping options open" and making sure he had a loophole large enough "to drive a Mack truck through" represented the essence of his management philosophy. While a case can be made for flexibility, progress requires choosing a direction from available options and committing to clearly defined outcomes. Political pressures and circumstances influenced his decisions far more than principle. Interestingly, this executive "taught" others to trust neither his words nor his actions.

Several key principles that serve as universal guides include integrity, accountability, excellence, respect, compassion, spirituality, service, unconditional love, a win-win conflict outcome, and quality. Carefully determine your own values to assure the appropriate fit. Values, especially in the context of individual or organizational missions, provide a powerful framework for quality decisions that make a difference.

Step 2. Identify your goals and interests— what do you want?

Stephen Covey, in his book *The Seven Habits of Highly Effective People* (1989), reminds us to "begin with the end in mind." By first picturing what we want to create, we can apply internal and external resources to realize that dream. Covey also reinforces the idea that "all things are created twice." What we first create in the mind is later transformed into reality. This step capitalizes on the principle that "we become what we think about" as a critical transformational strategy.

Often what we say we want is not at all what we do want! And sometimes we don't know what we want! For example, a person may say, "I want a deep, loving relationship." What's true is that she may really want to avoid getting hurt again! Another may say, "I want a red sports car." Instead, he may want to feel young again, may need more adventure in his life, or perhaps may want the car to attract attention. It is essential to be clear about what you really want before making a commitment. Be willing to look behind the surface reason for your more substantive motives. Seeking clarity at this point enables you to direct energy and resources to what is genuinely important.

With an open, conscious mind, ask:

- What one thing in my *personal* life could I change that would make a significant, positive, long-term difference?

- What one thing in my *professional* life could I change that would make a significant, positive, long-term difference?

Step 3. Create options to serve your values and goals.

Premature closure can be the root of many poor decisions and frequently the cause of broken commitments. Sometimes today's solutions become tomorrow's problems. Deciding too quickly on the basis of limited options results in pursuing an unsatisfactory course of action.

Before deciding, invent options that potentially serve your goals, interests, and values. Be willing to be creative and look for the second and third "right answer." Examine your criteria and conditions for including options to ensure that they support rather than limit your interests. Call upon your inner head-heart resources to work for you. Conscious application of these resources will make a difference.

Step 4. Select a course of action consistent with your values and goals.

Step 3 emphasized *creativity* in inventing options. We now apply the *critical thinking* process to narrow down those options and make a prudent choice. Applying principles, values, and decision-making criteria to the available options assists us in making a choice that maximizes results and increases our personal commitment to stick with the decision even during tough times.

In addition to using objective criteria and picturing the outcome, apply the decision-making "passion test." To what extent does the decision get your "internal juices" flowing? To what degree will it sustain your excitement level in the long run? Imagine this decision being tested under the most difficult of circumstances. Can you see yourself holding firm or bending with the prevailing wind? Consider also the best that could happen by fulfilling this commitment at a high level. Where do you place yourself on a long-term commitment scale of 0 to 10 related to converting this decision into reality? Are you prepared to do whatever it takes to make this happen? Pay careful attention to your response.

Step 5. Declare a position "publicly."

While some decisions are personal and private, most will become evident to others anyway. A powerful strategy that increases commitment and gains support requires you to take a "public" stance. Declaring a position to other key people in your life and committing publicly becomes a contract that elevates internal and external performance expectations. Creative stress works for you to produce the desired results.

Marriage ceremonies, Alcoholics Anonymous, and weight loss programs often tap into the power of public pronouncements to assist individuals in accomplishing goals. Often, other people will introduce resources that augment our own and assist in making a difference.

233

A word of caution, however. Not all individuals will support your goals. Committing to a decision publicly is likely to separate you from some people and expose you to criticism. Some personal goals are best made privately or shared only with those who will commit to unconditional support. Consider also the timing of when to share these goals with trusted associates. Depending on the nature of the commitment, some people may need to be involved early, while others can be advised after your decision is made.

Step 6. Convert your commitment into action—unpack your bags!

Now that you have gone through the essential preliminary steps, the real test is *action*. Transformation requires you to convert your commitment into tangible, specific behaviors. It also requires you to focus and let go of the other options you once considered to be viable. No more traveling bags. No more back doors left wide open for an easy escape. You have now committed to a direction. Unpack those bags *now* and do whatever it takes to convert that commitment into reality. This is your breakthrough moment.

So now what? *Who* is going to do *what* by *when?* Being clear about the big picture, your principles, and your values provides a context in which to take decisive, tangible action steps. Each conscious step brings you closer to your desired end state.

Apply the principle of "big-little-big." First, dream *big*. The problem, according to Bob Moawad (1985), is not having too large a goal and missing; it is having too small a goal and hitting! Second, take a focused series of *little* action steps that will bring you closer to the desired state. Words without actions are only empty promises. Converting your commitment into action transforms the agreement into reality. Third, ultimately experience your *big* dream! Celebrate successes while you learn from the transformational process. What would be different if your behavior followed your commitment?

Step 7. Evaluate the results: Celebrate successes and take corrective action when appropriate.

Apply this question as an ongoing test of progress: "Is what I am doing right now bringing me closer to or farther away from my commitment?" Pausing to get quiet inside will help you to draw on internal resources to answer this important question. In almost all cases, the answer to this question is within—you will know what needs to be done to make a difference.

How we behave when others who are affected by our decision are not present becomes an important measure of our commitment and a test of our integrity. Perhaps the most important person in our agreement can be seen in the mirror. Fudging on our commitment when others will not find out erodes our integrity and places that important goal farther away. Maintaining our commitment under difficult conditions becomes self-inspiring and accelerates our progress.

A useful strategy in maintaining momentum involves periodic assessment of results. Celebration of even small milestones kindles the spirit while encouraging even more progress. Likewise, self-correcting when we veer off course reinforces the integrity of our commitment while providing an opportunity to learn.

> ## "Effort fully releases its reward only after a person refuses to quit."
>
> Napoleon Hill

Commitment links an important desired future state with present behavior. Nothing of great significance occurs until you decide and put your internal will or commitment on the line. When you make the decision to act, the universe of resources responds, and you get results.

AWARENESS CHECKS

◑ What significant element in your personal or professional life can you change that will make a significant, positive difference?

◑ What commitments do your behaviors reflect?

◑ Are your choices bringing you closer to or farther from your commitments?

◑ What is the learning?

Following through on your commitment—punching through your barriers—becomes a breakthrough moment that converts challenges into results. What is trying to happen in your life right now? Are you ready for a breakthrough moment? Are you ready to commit and unpack your bags?

Integrity:
WALKING YOUR TALK!

"I am my message."

Gandhi

A wise nun I met some years ago said, "A value is only a theory until it is put into practice." Clearly, what you do speaks louder than your actions. Linking what you say with what you do becomes the essence of integrity. Consider two individuals, both of whom value charity. One talks of the importance of supporting charity; the other gives to charity. Which one actually values charity?

You cannot *not* influence others. You are always influencing others. *How* you influence them is the important question. You continually influence through your words and actions, even through your silence and inaction! Pastor Martin Niemoeller, a German

Lutheran minister, wrote after World War II of his own wake-up calls:

> In Germany, they came first for the Communists, and I didn't speak up because I wasn't a Communist. Then they came for the Jews, and I didn't speak up because I wasn't a Jew. They came for the trade unionists, and I didn't speak up because I wasn't a trade unionist. They came for the Catholics, and I didn't speak up because I was a Protestant. Then they came for me, and by that time no one was left to speak up . . .

You are always influencing. To influence with integrity—to walk your talk—means to:

- Do what you value—in a way that values others.

- Keep your agreements when the going gets tough.

- Keep your agreements even when the other person is *not* present.

The real test of our values and integrity is not when things are going well.
*The real test is when things are **not** going well.*

James Allen (1959) said: "Circumstances do not determine a man, they reveal him." Under adverse conditions, your real "stuff" tends to emerge. It is easy to support those who support you, to respect those who respect you, to love those who love you. The test of your values occurs when people do not support, love, or respect you. How do you behave under those conditions?

You are constantly teaching others how to behave toward you. Your words and behaviors are just representations of your internal experience. If your integrity is traded for expediency, you end up paying an enormous price in the process. Chipping away at your integrity also chips away at your sense of self-worth. Honoring your agreements, especially under difficult conditions, enhances your self-esteem while positively influencing others. Never yield to pressure—yield only to principle, advise Roger Fisher and William Ury (1983).

Adverse conditions present an opportunity to be influential. Consider Johnson & Johnson in the early 1980s. One of their products, Tylenol®, was tainted with cyanide and eight people died. This value-driven company immediately acted with integrity and removed all Tylenol products from retail shelves nationally. While this decision reportedly cost the company over $240 million, public confidence in their products was maintained if not increased. (How much is your integrity worth?) The company's products continue to enjoy strong consumer support. Notice what Johnson & Johnson taught the public through their actions. And notice the positive, *long-term* results for the company. Several recent studies have concluded that companies that function with integrity enjoy greater profits than those that trade integrity for short-term profits. Another paradox. Another wake-up call.

Honor the spirit of agreements.

Keeping agreements is one of the more significant ways by which you manifest your integrity. What do you teach others about the extent to which you honor your agreements? Gary Koyen, a friend and teacher, shared the following "levels of agreement" several years ago. I have since modified the agreement levels somewhat, yet his concept remains intact:

Levels of Agreement

Level 1	Minus agreement
Level 2	Neutral agreement
Level 3	Passive agreement

Level 4 Active agreement
Level 5 Commitment
Level 6 Zen intention

What do these levels of agreement mean?

Level 1. Minus Agreement

In these circumstances, we either say yes or say nothing at all when we intend to say no. Our words say one thing and our actions demonstrate another. In fact, individuals who function in level 1 are in active resistance by consciously or unconsciously fighting the agreement.

In organizations, for example, two kinds of meetings may occur: the *formal* meeting and the *parking lot* meeting. At the formal meeting, people tend to go along with the agreements or sit in silence. After the formal meeting, they gather in the parking lot and have the real meeting. Here they share what's really on their minds—what they think, feel, and want. In the parking lot, they complain about the decisions made by others. Called "organizational sabotage," these dysfunctional parking lot meetings erode trust and build communication barriers; then people wonder why trust levels and communication are so poor. If you participate in this kind of parking lot meeting, as either a listener or speaker, you contribute to the erosion of individual and organizational integrity.

WHILE I WAS FLYING EAST TO WORK with a client, a middle-aged man sitting next to me on the plane asked what kind of work I did. After I briefly described my work, he said, "Oh, let me tell you about my wife." Just what I wanted to hear! Story after story about their dysfunctional relationship. We were having a parking lot meeting at 35,000 feet! I finally asked the man if he had shared any of these feelings with his wife. "Are you kidding? If I talked with my wife about this, I would be in big trouble." I responded, "If you don't talk with your wife about these feelings, I think you will be in trouble." He looked puzzled.

240

Level 2. Neutral Agreement

"I don't care. It doesn't make any difference to me one way or the other." Individuals who make "neutral" agreements often use wishy-washy statements like this one. What an agreement! Obviously, the results will reflect this detached position. Relationship tension often results from such an "I don't care" attitude. If in fact the person really does not care, he or she can maintain integrity by stating this up front and relinquishing the decision to someone who does care about the situation.

Level 3. Passive Agreement

Suppose that you bump into someone you haven't seen for some time. After a bit of small talk, you suggest, "Why don't we get together for lunch sometime?" The other person smiles and says, "Good idea! I've got to run now. I'll give you a call sometime." What are the chances of "getting together for lunch sometime"? Slim to none. You have just entered into a passive agreement.

Level 4. Active Agreement

Consider the same situation acted on differently. You bump into someone you haven't seen for a while and suggest, "Why don't we get together for lunch sometime?" The other person smiles in agreement; you set a date, time, and place for lunch; and each of you marks it in your appointment book. What are the chances of "getting together for lunch sometime"? Very good! In fact, lunch with this person will probably happen. An active agreement has mutual clarity of *who* is going to do *what* by *when*.

Level 5. Commitment

At this level, what you want to do becomes the focus. In addition to clarifying who is going to do what by when, level 5 agreements **241** have an underlying intention to carry them out. At this level, your internal juices flow! Creativity flourishes. Things happen.

Suppose, for example, that you already have a level 4 agreement to get together with your friend for lunch. Then something comes up that you very much want to do at the same time as the luncheon appointment. Your values conflict. You call up your friend and say, "Something came up, and I will not be able to join you for lunch. Let's get together for lunch sometime later." Now where are you? Back to level 3—passive agreement. And you now can make a level 5 agreement to do what you want to do instead of the lunch. Notice how the hierarchy of agreements affects our performance.

Level 6. Zen Intention

People within our culture rarely practice agreements at the Zen intention depth. At this level, an inner knowingness communicates the intention that the agreement will be carried out. No questions. No excuses. It simply will happen. This level honors not only the content, but the *spirit* of the agreement. And the agreement will be carried out in spite of the most difficult of circumstances.

A Zen intention story told by Gary Koyen involves an old man in an Oriental village. The man delivered eggs every Tuesday to a neighboring village. One Tuesday, he carefully packed his eggs into his leather pouch and began his journey of several miles. Over the hill and down into the small village below walked the old man. To his dismay, however, he discovered that the village was under attack by a band of warriors. A woman on his egg delivery route had barricaded her windows and doors for protection from the ravages of the war outside. Suddenly, there was a knock at her door. She cautiously peered through the peephole, only to discover the egg man. She demanded, "What are you doing here? There's a war going on outside!" He responded calmly, "This is Tuesday. I deliver eggs on Tuesday." Zen intention. Keeping agreements. Functioning with integrity.

Doing business with some Oriental cultures can be a baffling experience for Americans. When they complete negotiations, Oriental businesspeople signal their agreement with a bow. This represents their Zen intention. American businesspeople immediately arrange for the agreement to be put in writing, witnessed by four people, notarized, and signed by both parties. The Oriental businesspeople are insulted. They have already given their Zen intention, and the written contract is considered to be a lesser form of agreement.

Be true to yourself to be true to others.

In our culture, most agreements between individuals and within organizations range from the *minus* through *passive* levels. It is no wonder that interpersonal trust levels are frequently issues at home and at work.

AWARENESS CHECKS

- At what level do you make most of your agreements?

- What would people at work and at home say about your level of agreements?

- What do you teach others about your agreements?

- What levels of agreement do you want from others? What levels are you willing to give?

- What is the learning?

Walking your talk and being true to yourself becomes the foundation of being true to others. Integrity, being *integrated,*   **243** links head and heart to produce higher results. Integrity integrates such important elements as being honest with yourself and others; talking straight; accepting accountability; delivering a safe, quality product; cleaning up your own messes; and treating others with respect.

By committing to make your words and actions fit your values, you begin making a difference in your own life and the lives of those around you. Integrity is walking your talk.

"This above all: to thine own self be true, and it must follow as the night the day, thou canst not then be false to any man."

William Shakespeare

Part 5

STAYING
AWAKE

Earth School:
TEACHERS COME IN
MANY FORMS

**"When the student is ready,
the teacher will appear."**

The Buddha

Airplanes are like flying classrooms of life. Jammed together in a self-contained environment, passengers are propelled through the air at 550 miles per hour. Although each is from a different walk of life and has a different purpose for flying, the entire group shares a common experience: sometimes a positive experience, sometimes not. This intense travel adventure often brings out people's "stuff." I am reminded of Mother Earth being propelled through space with billions of different people sharing a common experience. Each of us is independent yet interdependent as we travel together. Each of us is a student in Earth School.

WHILE TRAVELING ON A LONG CROSS-COUNTRY FLIGHT to Philadelphia one night, I was reading a book in preparation for working with a client. Sitting next to me was a grandmother with her seven-year-old grandson. She hated the kid! Granted, the boy was an active seven-year-old, yet *her* behavior was even more difficult for me. Every now and then, she would roll her eyes, swear, and slap him in the face. She was constantly scolding and complaining. I thought that she was one of the nastiest individuals I had ever experienced.

I didn't want to become involved with this woman while preparing for a sensitive interdepartmental conflict situation. Because every seat in the plane was occupied, however, moving was not an option. My internal agitation with this woman continued to increase. I already was involved!

I kept reading my book. A voice then said, "Sir!" As I was both reading and intentionally trying to shut her out, the voice did not fully register. Then I heard a more aggressive voice say, "*Sir!*" I closed my book, looked impatiently at her, and said, "Yes?" Her narrow eyes looked into mine and she demanded, "What time is it in Philadelphia?" Having already set my watch for East Coast time, I replied, "10:17." She then said, "Crap." Not "Thank you," but "*Crap!*" (Her actual word was a bit stronger, yet carried the same meaning.) I was now fully involved. My stomach churned, *my* eyes narrowed—and I wanted to assist her off the plane while still airborne!

I know better—it's not polite to push a grandmother out of an airplane. I still wanted to, though. My self-talk switched to high gear. "Eric, what do you tell your clients to do? Oh, yeah. *Pause.* Head-heart connection." After quieting down inside, I decided to go back to my book. I didn't want to talk with her. I wasn't going to make her change her crummy attitude, anyway.

There are no accidents. The book I was reading, Ken Keyes' *Handbook to Higher Consciousness* (1975), happened to open to a page I had already read. I had previously highlighted a paragraph in yellow and marked it with two stars in the margin. Two stars means that something is important to me—and that I need to pay attention to it. The messages from Ken Keyes in that marked paragraph and several others provided yet another wake-up call:

> Everyone and everything around you is your teacher. . . . A person for whom you feel little attraction is probably your most helpful teacher. . . . You will grow faster by experiencing someone that you usually would have excluded from your life. . . . Expand your love, your consciousness, and your loving compassion by experiencing everything that everyone does or says as though you had done or said it. . . . A conscious being knows that life always works best when we operate from a loving space that lets us receive and experience other people (no matter what they do or say) as no different from ourselves.

Come on now! This wicked, mean lady is a *teacher?* "*. . . no different from ourselves?*" I am in resistance. What can I learn from her? I don't even like her. I am impatient with her. I feel very judgmental toward her. I don't care for her values. And I still want to push her out of the plane!

What can I learn from her? It's time to pause and get that head-heart connection. This lady *is* a teacher—an important teacher to me! In fact, she mirrors my internal experience. She is impatient with her grandson. I am impatient with her. She is judgmental toward him. I am judgmental toward her. She loves him conditionally. I love her conditionally. She wants him to change. I want her to change. She wants to get rid of him. I want to get rid of her. She is no different from me, this fellow traveler of mine in Earth School. With no other seats available on the plane, the universe sent a message I needed to hear through this grandmother. Another teachable moment. Another wake-up call!

"Those having torches will pass them on to others."

Plato   **249**

IN A SEMINAR I ATTENDED taught by Dr. Elisabeth Kubler-Ross, she shared an inspirational story about one of her most important life's teachers. As you may recall, Kubler-Ross has been one of the more influential individuals in assisting health-care professionals to deal with death and dying. As a young intern on a cancer ward years ago, she saw the difficulty of both staff and patients in dealing directly with the issues of death and dying. The patients needed to talk about dying, and the professional staff resisted exploring such sensitive issues, because the pain and discomfort were too great. Hiding within the white smocks of professional detachment became far easier than facing mortality.

After some months on the cancer ward, Kubler-Ross noticed that a particular African-American housekeeper appeared to gain an unusually positive rapport with terminal patients; the professional staff, conversely, found it difficult to relate to them. Whenever she cleaned their rooms, the attitude of patients appeared to be more positive, and they enjoyed a greater sense of inner peace. Kubler-Ross began spying on the housekeeper to discover her connection with them. Finally, she confronted the housekeeper, asking what she was doing with the patients. Feeling highly intimidated, the housekeeper responded to the physician's challenge by saying, "Nothing! Nothing! I'm just doing my job cleaning the room." Recognizing her tenseness, Kubler-Ross put her at ease. A beautiful friendship was ultimately to form—and important learning for Kubler-Ross.

At that time in the African-American culture, dying family members stayed home rather than being sent to hospitals and nursing homes. They could not afford to be sent away during their final days. Death was as natural as the life process itself. Both adults and children were exposed to dying and death. They learned how to deal with it openly and naturally. They learned to talk with the dying and to share their feelings. They experienced life leaving the body. They knew of these things as participants.

Many health-care professionals do not share that cultural background. It's awkward and uncomfortable to be around the dying. What do you say? Avoidance seems to be easier. Yet the need to connect is even stronger during those final days.

The African-American housekeeper became one of the most important life teachers to Kubler-Ross. As a student of the housekeeper, Kubler-Ross later became an important teacher herself as she helped others to deal positively, both profession- ally and personally, with dying and death. What a wonderful gift that housekeeper has given us through a physician who was open enough to receive an important wake-up call from an otherwise unlikely teacher.

Look for the teachable moment.

What if you looked on each person and each situation as a teachable moment—a wake-up call? This ancient Oriental philosophy of looking for the learning be- comes a powerful tool of lifelong growth. And it can make a significant, positive difference in your own life and in the lives of your fellow travelers.

Ever since the 1987 "grandmother-in-the-airplane wake-up call," I have been stretching myself to look on each person as a teacher, just as the grandmother was an important teacher for me. What a gold mine! And what fun. With each person, ask, "What can I learn from this person?" With each situation, ask, "What can I learn from this situation?" Get quiet inside—make the head-heart connection—and listen for the response. Often the learning is about you—your strengths and your stretches; sometimes it is about others and sometimes it is about life. Look for the positive learning and be willing to put your own stuff aside. Drawing from the philosophy of an old cowboy: "With all this manure around, there's got to be a pony somewhere!" Look for the pony.

All of us are teachers and students in the journey of life in Earth School. Who are your teachers? What are you learning? What limits, if any, do you place on your teachers—either who they are or what they have to teach? Are there certain individu- als or groups from whom you are unwilling to learn? Usually that **251** which you resist contains within it your greatest opportunity for growth and development. What are the benefits and costs of limiting your teachers?

AWARENESS CHECKS

◖ Who are your teachers?

◖ What are you teaching others? (Remember, you are *their* teacher!) What are they learning from your words and actions?

◖ If other people "caught" your attitudes and behaviors (which they do), what would this world be like?

◖ What is the learning?

Your teachers come in many forms, and each provides an opportunity for higher consciousness and greater life fulfillment. Look for the learning in your Earth School experience.

The Rewards of Mastery:

LIFELONG LEARNING

"Unless you try to do something beyond what you have already mastered, you will never grow."

Ralph Waldo Emerson

Shape your future or be shaped by it! Either you control your own destiny, or external forces will take charge. Mastery, the active choice of being the very best you can be, makes a profound life difference. Commitment to mastery positions you to both determine your destination and experience a higher-quality journey. Those who invest significantly in themselves generally experience much higher levels of life and career fulfillment. Yet few people commit to meaningful self-development. That baffles me.

> *"Every man is ignorant—*
> *just on different subjects."*
>
> Will Rogers

Twenty-three million adults, or about 15 percent of the American work force, are functional illiterates. As consumers press for higher standards of service and product performance, even entry-level positions require increasing knowledge and skills. Under these demanding conditions, the American educational system has been allowed to slip to number *twelve* in the world and appears to still be declining! Talk about "wake-up calls"! Many companies in corporate America can no longer rely on high school or even college graduates to perform at expected levels. U.S. companies spend more than $210 billion annually on training and development just to keep pace with present demands.

Executive, technical, and professional levels require more brainpower as well. Even farming and garbage disposal have now become high tech! Informational half-life is three years in the computer field and five years in the medical field. This means that if I were a computer expert, approximately one-half of what I now know would be obsolete in three years! And that's assuming that what I now know is current. In the medical profession, one-half of what your physician knows will be obsolete in five years. What if your surgeon hasn't participated in continuing education for the last ten years? Does that provocative thought get your adrenaline flowing?

Stephen Covey (1989) explores the critical self-renewal principle of "sharpening the saw." He describes an individual who is working feverishly to cut down a large tree. Another person, observing his hard work, asks him why he doesn't take a break to sharpen the saw. "I don't have time to sharpen the saw," replies the worker. "I'm too busy sawing." To what extent are you so busy sawing that you don't have time to renew yourself physically, mentally, spiritually, and professionally? To what extent are you pausing to keep your relationships fresh and alive? If you don't pause for systematic self-renewal in these important life areas, you can count on receiving wake-up calls that will demand immediate attention.

If you don't develop your competitive edge, your competitors will edge you out!

The late Earl Nightingale, "dean of personal and professional growth," observed that only one hour of study per day in your chosen field of interest places you at the top in only three years, positions you to be a national authority in five years, and makes you an internationally renowned expert in seven years! Yet the average American adult reads less than one book per year. And 58 percent of the American population never read another nonfiction book cover to cover following their high school years.

A working adult spends between 500 and 1,000 hours per year behind the wheel of a car. This equates to 12½ to 25 *work weeks* per year. Is this lost time or a golden opportunity for you? What if, as part of your lifelong learning commitment, you listened to audiotapes in your chosen field during this time? What if you gained one or two new ideas per day through this process? What if you actively applied these ideas? Increasing your value pays dividends to your employer—and ultimately to you.

If you don't develop your competitive edge, your competitors will edge you out. Tom Peters reports that "everything is being smartened up." Smarter design, products, service, distribution, marketing, and research are now required just to keep your hat in the ring! The ability to learn faster than your competitors, claims Peters, may well be your most significant strategy to maintain that coveted competitive edge. The Japanese term *kaizen* means constant, incremental improvement. Attention to innovation and quality has positioned Japanese products to be the competitive leaders in the world market. The same principle can apply to your personal and professional positioning.

Brian Tracy (1989a) appropriately concludes that "you are paid exactly what you are worth—no more, no less." If you are not paid enough, then commit to increasing your value. Commit to mastery. Commit to being so good at what you do that when a special need arises, others think of *you* as the resource. People are willing to pay for what they value. Practicing *kaizen* is a key strategy to get there.

AWARENESS CHECKS

- What is your competitive edge and what specifically are you doing to enhance your personal and professional mastery?

- What are you doing to position yourself to be an expert in your field?

- On a scale of 0 to 10, to what extent are you fulfilled with your present status?

- To what extent are you valued by your boss and peers? By your competitors?

- What is the learning?

Career extinction follows complacency.

At seminars I conduct, I am frequently approached by individuals who say, "I want to do what you do. What steps can I take to get there?" This feels good, and I am certainly interested in contributing to their success. Yet some interesting dynamics occur in the moments that follow. I usually get a sense of whether these individuals are "flirters" or "lovers." Flirters shoot for minimums. They look for shortcuts. They want sensational results without a commitment. They don't unpack their bags and they keep the back door open. When I talk with them about developing their educational levels, attending seminars, reading books, listening to tapes, studying peak performers, and being willing to endure little or no income in the initial years, they back off quickly. The seminars are "too expensive." The time commitment is too great. The risks are overwhelming. In some form, they invariably ask, "Are there any shortcuts?"

Then there are the lovers. These are the passionate people, the people who are willing to do *whatever it takes.* They intrinsically feel that they are worth the investment. They have a dream. They take action. They invest in themselves. They contribute. And they get results. The others just wonder why good things don't "happen" to them and complain about their condition.

Life doesn't just happen; we create the results we experience. What are you creating in your life? Your career? Your relationships? If you don't like what you are getting back in life, examine what you are putting out.

"It's what you learn after you know it all that counts."

John Wooden,
Former UCLA basketball coach

Never become satisfied with your personal and professional development. Complacency becomes the first step toward career extinction, for both individuals and organizations.

I AM REMINDED OF THE STORY OF MARY, a patient in a mental health facility. Mary was obsessed with collecting towels. Other patients frequently were frustrated when they returned from their showers only to find their towel racks empty; Mary had visited. Every effort to break her of this behavioral pattern was unsuccessful. Her insatiable need drove her to creatively collect every towel on the ward.

Out of desperation, her psychiatrist finally wrote the following order for the nurses: "Every fifteen minutes, deliver a package of towels to Mary's room." The first package of fifty towels was delivered, and Mary was ecstatic. Fifteen minutes later, another package of towels arrived. Then another and another. She was in "towel heaven"; she'd found the mother lode right there in the hospital. Soon her room resembled the hospital laundry supply room. Eventually, she could hardly move about in her room. Finally she said, "No more towels." Her need had been satisfied. Once it is satisfied, the inner drive to change and innovate diminishes. *Dissatisfaction,* on the other hand, can be one of our strongest allies.

In mastering the art of karate, one progresses through a series of steps before reaching the coveted "black belt." At each stage, the athlete must master the fundamentals before advancing to the next belt. Mastering the fundamentals requires patience, persistence, and practice. Rather than directing your competitive energy to beating others, emphasize being the very best you can be. Not better than the others, just the best you can be.

John Wooden, the revered UCLA basketball coach, insisted that each of his players repeatedly practice the fundamentals. While some of the players initially resisted practicing what they already did well, mastery of the fundamentals proved to be the competitive edge on the court. Wooden focused on excellence, not winning. Yet his team had more consecutive winning seasons than any other in the history of college basketball. Before advancing to your next step, ask yourself to what extent you have committed to mastering your current level of performance.

*"I do the very best I know how—
the very best I can; and I mean
to keep doing so until the end."*

Abraham Lincoln

IN THE 1988 OLYMPIC GAMES IN KOREA, a swimmer clearly led in one of the events. With the coveted Gold Medal only two meters away, the lead swimmer felt that the pressure was off, so he coasted. The number two swimmer, aware of the opportunity, kicked it in. By only a fingertip and one one-hundredth of a second, the "number two" swimmer gained the lead and claimed the Gold Medal. Another wake-up call. Another one of life's teachable moments.

When it comes to development, don't cheat yourself. By committing 2 to 5 percent of your annual income and 5 percent of your time to your personal and professional development, you will position yourself to be a recognized leader in your field. When you increase your value, others attribute more value to you. Both your journey and your destination will be more fulfilling as a result of that life choice.

When you are aware of the opportunity for mastery and are confronted with a choice point, what do you choose for yourself? No one else can or will do your work for you.

You and Your Oxygen Mask:

TAKING CARE OF YOURSELF

"We cannot be a source of strength unless we nurture our own strength."

M. Scott Peck

As a frequent passenger on commercial airliners, I find that flying has become routine, even automatic. I rarely pay attention to the flight attendants as preflight emergency instructions are announced. I know all that stuff.

It's funny what occurs when we "know all that stuff." We stop listening. We stop paying attention. We stop learning. Then we have a wake-up call.

On an airliner about two years ago, flight attendants gave their usual preflight emergency instructions: "If there is a sudden decrease in cabin pressure, the oxygen masks will automatically drop down. Place the yellow mask over your nose and mouth and the oxygen will automatically flow. If you are an adult traveling with someone who may need assistance, attach the mask to yourself first before you assist that other person." This time, the words took on new meaning.

Imagine a flight with a three-year-old child seated next to you. An inflight emergency occurs. The oxygen masks drop down, but the child's mask is out of her reach. With fear in her eyes and tears coming down her cheeks, she helplessly looks up at you. She obviously needs your help and support. With the oxygen masks dangling in front of the two of you, a choice point is at hand. To whom do you attach the mask first? The child or you? The natural inclination may be to attach the oxygen mask to the child first. Yet the instructions were to attach the mask to yourself first. It sounds so selfish!

A good reason exists for attaching the mask to yourself first. By taking care of yourself first, you are able to be there to support the child. If you don't place the oxygen mask on yourself first, both you and the child are placed at risk.

"Love is the overflow of what you have after self-love."

David Viscott

By serving our own needs first, we are better able to serve others. This is a difficult concept for some of us! In fact, by taking care of ourselves physically, emotionally, and spiritually, we are able to provide an even higher level of service to others. Loving others starts with loving ourselves. The quality of our relationships with others often mirrors the quality of our self-love. Learning to be our own best friend becomes a big stretch for some of us.

You may generate resistance to this concept. If so, be willing to pause and look for the learning. Let's go further.

Suppose that your philosophy is to love and serve others. While this is a noteworthy philosophy, the costs can be great for both yourself and others when you ignore your own needs. By meeting the needs of others at your expense, you begin to build relationship tension under the surface. Eventually, feelings of resentment may start creeping in. You begin to ask, "What about my needs?" "Why do their needs always seem to be met, while I end up with the leftovers?"

As we seek to place the oxygen mask on others, we may ignore our own needs. We have successfully taught others that we are here to serve them. Sometimes we even resist their efforts to be of service to *us* because "our duty" is to be there for them! Test this out. When other people want to give you something or do something for you, how do you respond? Do you resist or discount their efforts? What are you teaching them in the process? Pay attention to how you act when you are on the receiving end. Sometimes we teach others not to give to us, then become resentful when our unexpressed needs are not met.

> *"Ask, and you will receive;*
> *seek, and you will find;*
> *knock, and the door will be opened to you."*
>
> Matthew 7:7

Emotional health requires a flow of oxygen, too. Learn to let others apply an oxygen mask to you at a time of need—and to let them know directly what would be most helpful. A client of mine has made it her practice to be of service to her family to such an extent that her own needs go unfulfilled, and her oxygen tank becomes empty. One of the few things she wanted from her husband was to be told more often how much he loved and appreciated her. After building up her courage, she eventually asked for what she wanted. He quickly responded by saying, "OK, I love you." She immediately retorted, "Well, that doesn't count. I told you to say that." Even though his skill was not very high, a positive intention backed up his words. Yet she discounted the words rather than accepting and building on the effort. History was repeated, and the same dysfunctional cycle prevailed. Pay attention to how you create the results you experience in life. To have a more fulfilling life, learn to clarify, ask for, and accept what you need and want.

Quality relations require nurturing of both the self and others. Of the *self?* Yes, of the self as well. How are you taking care of your relationship with yourself? To what extent are you loving yourself? The quality of your external relationships reflects the quality relationship you have with yourself. Individuals who nurture themselves enhance their capacity to develop quality external relationships.

Pay attention to the relationship you have with yourself. Individuals with low self-esteem tend to have poor relationships with others. Those with high self-esteem tend to have more meaningful relationships. Quality relationships start from within. Are you consciously developing this relationship, or are you participating in another sleepwalking experience?

Put on your oxygen mask.

Let's apply the oxygen mask concept. Recall a time in your life when you made a mistake. A big mistake. (You have made at least *one,* haven't you?) Re-create and experience how you felt. What was your self-talk like? Was it something like: "I can't believe I did that!" or "What a stupid mistake"?

How would it feel if, when you made a mistake, your boss, spouse, or parent said, "I can't believe you did that" or "What a stupid mistake"? Notice how different it feels when someone else says those same words to us. Our feelings get hurt and we become defensive. Our self-esteem suffers. Instead of making a mistake, we *become* a mistake. Experience that fully.

Now, bring your best friend to mind. Imagine that your best friend made the same mistake you did. How would you talk to this special person? Note both what you would say and how you might communicate the message. Would your tone of voice differ from the way you talked to yourself when you made the same mistake? You bet! You would probably be more accepting, empathetic, supporting, and understanding with your best friend. The chances are that you would say something like: "It's going to be OK; we all make mistakes," "This is a good learning opportunity," or "How can I support you?" You would care enough to offer a positive perspective, to be encouraging, and to help your friend to look for the learning. Notice how you treat your friend and be willing to apply this behavior to yourself.

Does a difference exist between how you treat yourself and how you treat your best friend when you make a mistake? Most of us are much tougher on ourselves than we are on others. What if you talked to others the way you talk to yourself when you make a mistake? No one would tolerate that kind of abuse! You probably wouldn't have any friends left. *Alone at last* becomes the result. If you cannot support yourself, if you cannot be on your own team, if you cannot nurture yourself, who else will support you? Who will want to be on your team? Pay attention to your self-talk. The whole concept of building quality relationships starts from within and becomes externalized. Loving others unconditionally starts with loving yourself unconditionally.

Assignment time. Ugh! Yet this assignment is optional. Ahhh! (Note your response when it comes to self-development assignments.) For the next twenty-one days (the time during which it takes to develop a habit), pay attention to your self-talk. Listen to how you take care of yourself. Catch yourself doing things right—or even approximately right. Acknowledge yourself. If you make a mistake (and you should be making plenty of them to get the most out of life), treat yourself as if you were your own best friend. When you first notice destructive self-talk, interrupt the pattern and self-correct. Draw on your internal resources to be of service to you as you would rely on your best friend. Be accepting, empathetic, supporting, and understanding. Look for the learning, let go, and move on. Counsel yourself as you would your best friend.

This internal coaching facilitates the growth process. Your self-esteem, consisting of feeling both competent and worthy, continues to strengthen. By modeling being on your own team, you enhance your effectiveness. In the process, you become what you are encouraging others to become. You get a double bonus!

Learn to apply the oxygen mask to yourself, and experience how much more you ultimately will be able to give to both yourself and others.

AWARENESS CHECKS

To what extent do you meet the needs of:

- Self?
- Others?

In serving self and others, do you put your own oxygen mask on first?

To what extent are you loving yourself?

What is the learning here?

26

Making It Stick:

THE BLIP THEORY

*"If you don't do something differently,
you'll end up where you are headed."*

Gary Koyen

So you want to make changes in your life. Converting wake-up calls into positive action requires courage and commitment. A part of you probably experiences excitement about clarifying goals and taking action. If you are like the rest of us, another part may experience fear, resistance, or complacency. Internal conflicts such as this play a major role in determining whether the changes stick in the long run. Which part will win—the part that wants to change or the part that doesn't?

Perhaps you have reached the decision to do things differently in an effort to produce even better results in such important areas as your career, relationships, finances, health, or even spiritual connection. If so, I applaud your decision. Now is the time to act—to move out of your comfort zone and get results. Until they have been applied, the lessons have not really been learned. And those lessons will return.

"Once you label me, you negate me."

Søren Kierkegaard

Making changes puts us against our stuff. Sometimes we put ourselves in a box labeled "This is who I am," or others put us in a box labeled "This is who you are." Self-imposed or other-imposed limits can be highly restrictive. Internal barriers to growth, our fears and negative self-talk are intensified through criticism from external sources. And it's tough to get out of the box.

Eventually we decide to move out of our box—to move beyond our "limitations." I call this "blipping out." Stimulated by a wake-up call, a conscious choice to grow and develop, or some traumatic life event, we start on our growth journey. "Blipping out" of our box involves leaving the familiarity of our comfort zone. And the breakthrough moment assists us in beginning a new journey.

Entering the blip or growth zone, we simultaneously experience excitement and fear. Our skill levels may not match our positive intentions. Our confidence and competence are usually a bit shaky. We begin asking, "Why am I putting myself through this?" We question our competence, experience feelings of discomfort, and criticize ourselves for our lack of perfection. Under these conditions, we may conclude that the changes are not worth the effort. Retreating to the familiar becomes a more attractive option than dealing with our "stuff"—even when old behavioral patterns do not work well for us.

THE BLIP THEORY

**This is how I see myself,
or how others see me.**

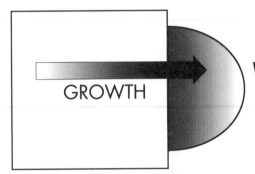

**When I grow, I "blip out"
by moving into new,
unfamiliar territory.**

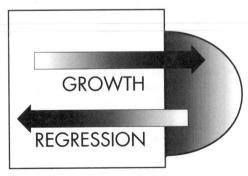

**If I am criticized in my
blip zone, I tend to
retreat to the familiar.**

In addition to self-criticism, criticism by others occurs as we grow, unskillfully at first, into our blip zone. Other people point out our flaws, criticize our lack of skill, question our motives, and wonder what's going on with us.

As we change, other people experience their own discomfort. At least they understood and knew what to expect with our old patterns of behavior. They knew "the old devil." They don't have a clue what the "new devil" is going to be like and how the changes in us will affect them. Even if they have previously encouraged us to change our behaviors, when we actually follow through with these changes, they become confused, scared, and critical. The result? We retreat to the familiar. We don't have enough encouragement to continue in what is already uncomfortable new territory for us. We go back to our old ways.

"All things are difficult before they are easy."

John Norley

IN MY FORMER CAREER IN HOSPITAL ADMINISTRATION, I received feedback several times from the night nursing staff expressing concern that they didn't know me. They had memos with my name on them and had seen pictures of me in internal publications, yet they didn't know *me*. The message from the nurses was "Why don't you come up and see us sometime?" At the time, I was working an average of sixty-five hours a week. Coming in in the middle of the night on top of that work schedule seemed a bit much. Yet communicating with the night staff was important.

I decided to take action—to "blip out." I made an appointment with the night nursing supervisor to circulate on the floors with her starting at 3:00 A.M. How do you suppose the nurses, who requested that I meet them, treated me? Half of them attacked: "Why are you here? What's wrong? Why are you spying

270

on us? Why did it take you so long to come up to meet us? Why don't you feel that we are as important as the day staff?" The other half of the nurses avoided me. When they saw me enter their hallway, there was a flurry of white uniforms as they grabbed clipboards and dashed off into patients' rooms. What they were doing with those patients in the middle of the night was beyond me.

How do you suppose I felt when I was treated this way by the nurses? To what extent do you think I was encouraged to continue "blipping out"? Outside of my comfort zone, my anxiety level rose and my desire to continue diminished. Fortunately, I realized that trust levels were low and I needed to continue returning at night to build positive relationships with the nurses. Eventual success in building bridges occurred in spite of their lack of initial support for my "blipping out."

Rewarding movement rather than criticizing unskilled behavior encourages continued growth.

As we grow and develop—entering into our blip zone—sometimes others won't let us out of the box they created for us. By focusing on our limitations and past performance, they do not notice our current growth and development. In some organizations, sadly, leaving becomes the only way that people can grow and develop. They move on to another organization where no history and no boxes exist and a fresh starting place becomes available. In a new setting, "blipping out" can occur without other people even knowing! Having no basis for comparison, our new colleagues consider our "blip" behavior to be routine. A new environment provides safety to experiment with new growth behaviors.

Organizations cannot afford to keep people contained. Nor can they afford to unconsciously discourage growth. The same **271** is true of relationships. When one individual grows, the other may feel threatened and wonder, "How will this new behavior affect our relationship?" Frustration and relationship tension sets in when growth is not acknowledged. The result? If a key person will not let us out of our box, a difficult choice is presented: leaving the relationship or staying in the same place and feeling resentful. The costs of keeping people in boxes are great. Another option, obviously, requires us to work through our collective "stuff" with caring straight talk. Yet even this direct approach involves both individuals moving out of their comfort zone to deal with the issues.

"Catch people doing something approximately right."

Ken Blanchard

Wake up! Never criticize a learner—even yourself. Never seek out the flaws as someone grows. Look for ways to acknowledge and encourage growth in others and in yourself. Criticizing others as they grow, or not acknowledging their growth, encourages them to retreat to the familiar, maintain their old patterns, or leave. We cannot afford to stifle the growth of others at work or at home. And we cannot afford to stifle our own growth.

In a seminar I attended, Ken Blanchard, coauthor of *The One Minute Manager* (1981), told a story related to supporting others as they grow. He asked, "How do you teach a killer whale to jump over a thirty-foot rope?" Since none of us were experts in training killer whales, he went on to describe two methods. One approach involves going out into the ocean with two boats, stringing a rope between the boats, getting a megaphone, finding a killer whale, and yelling, "Jump!" The results are fairly predictable. The chances are slim that a whale will follow the command.

The other way, Blanchard explained, requires capturing a killer whale and placing it in a large training tank. The first step, playing with the whale in the tank, communicates that you mean no harm to this gentle creature. You develop rapport and provide safety to create a supportive learning environment. Next, a rope is strung between two points under water. When the whale swims over the rope, a reward follows. There is no reward if the whale swims under the rope.

Now, it's no big deal when a whale swims over a submerged rope. Not too many people would be willing to pay admission only to hear an announcer exclaim: "Shamu just swam over the rope, folks!" Swimming over a submerged rope, according to Blanchard, is doing it "approximately right"—not a thirty-foot jump, but *approximately right*. By catching the whale doing something approximately right (blipping out!), we encourage its continued journey to the big event. Eventually the whale progresses to the spectacular thirty-foot jump.

The same concept applies to humans. When we nurture the growth of ourself and others, we can make a positive difference, and our relationships will strengthen. Assisting others to grow in their life journey can be a wonderful gift—both to them and to yourself. What if individuals, in both organizational and home environments, provided safety and encouragement for others to experiment with new growth behaviors? What if you committed to creating giants out of yourself and others through empowering the growth process? What if you nurtured "blipping out" with yourself and others?

"Things do not change; we change."

Henry David Thoreau

Making changes starts from the inside. The more aware you are, the more choices you create. Converting wake-up calls into positive life results is the difference that makes a difference. Now that you have explored the growth principles and strategies outlined in this book, you are at a new choice point where you can enhance the quality of life for yourself and those around you. Commit to taking charge of your life at an even higher level. And be prepared to experience more fulfilling, joyful results.

AWARENESS CHECKS

- Where in your life are you "blipping out"?
- Where in your life are you holding back?
- What if you committed to creating giants out of yourself and others at an even higher level?
- What is the learning here?

---

*"If not me, then who?
If not now, then when?"*

Paraphrase of an
ancient Jewish teaching

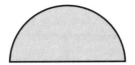

BIBLIOGRAPHY

Many creative minds have contributed to the development of this book. While *Wake-Up Calls* provides a fresh perspective, this effort represents a synergistic composite of ideas dating back several thousands of years. Some of the more contemporary literature that influenced my thinking includes, but is not limited to, the following works. I wish to acknowledge these sources in addition to the many life teachers who have made a difference in my life.

Allen, James. *As a Man Thinketh.* New York: Grosset and Dunlap, 1959.

Bandler, Richard, and John Grinder. *Frogs into Princes.* Moab, Utah: Real People Press, 1979.

Bandler, Richard, and John Grinder. *Reframing.* Moab, Utah: Real People Press, 1980.

Bethel, Sheila Murray. *Making a Difference.* New York: Putnam, 1990.

Blanchard, Kenneth, and Spencer Johnson. *The One Minute Manager.* New York: Berkley Books, 1981.

Blanchard, Kenneth, and Robert Lorber. *Putting the One Minute Manager to Work.* New York: Berkley Books, 1984.

Block, Peter. *The Empowered Manager: Positive Political Skills at Work.* San Francisco: Jossey-Bass, 1987.

Bloomfield, Harold H., and Sirah Vettese. *Joy! The Dynamics of Inner Success.* Chicago: Nightingale-Conant (Audiotape), 1986.

Branden, Nathaniel. *Honoring the Self.* Los Angeles: Jeremy P. Tarcher, 1983.

Brooks, Michael. *Instant Rapport.* New York: Warner Books, 1989.

Buscaglia, Leo. *Living, Loving and Learning.* New York: Fawcett Columbine, 1982.

Byham, William C. *Zapp! The Lightning of Empowerment.* New York: Harmony Books, 1988.

Campbell, Joseph. *The Power of Myth.* New York: Doubleday, 1988.

Cathcart, Jim, and Tony Alessandra. *Relationship Strategies.* Chicago: Nightingale-Conant (Audiotape), 1984.

Cohen, Alan. *Joy Is My Compass.* Somerset, N.J.: Alan Cohen Productions, 1990.

Cohen, Alan. *Rising in Love: The Journey into Light.* Somerset, N.J.: Alan Cohen Productions, 1983.

Coit, Lee. *Listening.* South Laguna, Calif.: Swan Publishing, 1985.

Cosby, Bill. *Fatherhood.* New York: Berkley Books, 1986.

Cosby, Bill. *Love and Marriage.* New York: Doubleday, 1989.

Covey, Stephen R. *The Seven Habits of Highly Effective People.* New York: Simon & Schuster, 1989.

Dass, Ram, and Paul Gorman. *How Can I Help?* New York: Knopf, 1985.

Dunnette, Marvin D. (Ed.). *Handbook of Industrial and Organizational Psychology.* Chicago: Rand McNally, 1976.

Dyer, Wayne. *Choosing Your Own Greatness.* Chicago: Nightingale-Conant (Audiotape), 1985.

Dyer, Wayne. *Gifts from Eykis.* New York: Pocket Books, 1983.

Dyer, Wayne. *The Sky's the Limit.* New York: Pocket Books, 1980.

Dyer, Wayne. *Transformation.* Chicago: Nightingale-Conant (Audiotape), 1987.

Dyer, Wayne. *You'll See It When You Believe It.* New York: William Morrow, 1989.

Ellsworth, Sterling, and Richard G. Ellsworth. *Getting to Know the Real You.* Salt Lake City, Utah: Deseret Book Company, 1981.

Fisher, Roger, and William Ury. *Getting to Yes.* New York: Penguin Books, 1983.

Fulgrum, Robert. *All I Really Needed to Know I Learned in Kindergarten.* New York: Villard Books, 1989.

Garfield, Charles. *Peak Performance.* Chicago: Nightingale-Conant (Audiotape), 1983.

Garfield, Charles. *Peak Performers: The New Heroes of American Business.* New York: William Morrow, 1986.

Gawain, Shakti. *Creative Visualization.* San Rafael, Calif.: New World Library, 1978.

Gawain, Shakti, and Laurel King. *Living in the Light.* San Rafael, Calif.: New World Library, 1986.

Greenwald, Jerry. *Creative Intimacy.* New York: Jove Publications, 1979.

Grinder, John, and Richard Bandler. *Trance-formations.* Moab, Utah: Real People Press, 1981.

Hanley, John. *Lifespring.* New York: Simon & Schuster, 1989.

Heider, John. *The Tao of Leadership.* Toronto: Bantam, 1986.

Hendricks, Gay, and Kathlyn Hendricks. *Conscious Loving.* New York: Bantam Books, 1990.

Hickman, Craig R. *Mind of a Manager—Soul of a Leader.* New York: Wiley, 1990.

Hickman, Craig R., and Michael A. Silva. *Creating Excellence.* New York: New American Library, 1984.

James, Eliott. *Living a Balanced Life*. Atlanta: Dhamma Books, 1990.

James, Jennifer. *Success Is the Quality of Your Journey*. New York: Newmarket Press, 1986.

James, Jennifer. *Windows*. New York: Newmarket Press, 1987.

Keyes, Ken. *Handbook to Higher Consciousness*. Coos Bay, Oreg.: Love Line Books, 1975.

Keyes, Ken. *The Hundredth Monkey*. Coos Bay, Oreg.: Vision Books, 1987.

Keyes, Ken. *Prescriptions for Happiness*. Coos Bay, Oreg.: Love Line Books, 1981.

Keyes, Ken. *Taming Your Mind*. Coos Bay, Oreg.: Love Line Books, 1989.

Keyes, Ken, and Penny Keyes. *The Power of Unconditional Love*. Coos Bay, Oreg.: Love Line Books, 1990.

Laborde, Genie Z. *Influencing with Integrity*. Palo Alto, Calif.: Syntony, 1984.

McCormack, Mark H. *What They Don't Teach You at Harvard Business School*. Toronto: Bantam Books, 1984.

McMaster, Michael, and John Grinder. *Precision: A New Approach to Communication*. Beverly Hills, Calif.: Precision Models, 1980.

McWilliams, John-Roger, and Peter McWilliams. *Life 101: Everything We Wish We Had Learned About Life in School—But Didn't*. Los Angeles: Prelude Press, 1990.

McWilliams, Peter, and John-Roger McWilliams. *You Can't Afford the Luxury of a Negative Thought*. Los Angeles: Prelude Press, 1989.

Miller, Lawrence. *Winning Through Teamwork*. Chicago: Nightingale-Conant (Audiotape), 1984.

Millman, Dan. *Way of the Peaceful Warrior*. Tiburon, Calif.: H. J. Kramer, 1980.

Moawad, Bob. *Increasing Human Effectiveness II: Managing the Rapids of Change*. Tacoma, Wash.: Edge Learning Institute (Audiotape), 1989.

Moawad, Bob. *Unlocking Your Potential*. Chicago: Nightingale-Conant (Audiotape), 1985.

Muggeridge, Malcolm. *Something Beautiful for God*. Great Britain: The Mother Teresa Committee, 1971.

Nightingale, Earl. *Success Series*. Chicago: Nightingale-Conant (Audiotape), 1981.

Peck, M. Scott. *The Road Less Travelled*. New York: Simon & Schuster, 1978.

Peters, Thomas J., and Robert H. Waterman. *In Search of Excellence*. New York: Harper and Row, 1982.

Peters, Tom, and Nancy Austin. *A Passion for Excellence*. New York: Random House, 1985.

Powell, John. *Unconditional Love*. Allen, Tex.: Argus Communications, 1978.

Powell, John. *Why Am I Afraid to Tell You Who I Am?* Allen, Tex.: Tabor Publishing, 1969.

Robbins, Anthony. *Personal Power*. Irwindale, Calif.: Robbins Research International (Audiotape), 1989.

Robbins, Anthony. *Unlimited Power*. New York: Fawcett Columbine, 1986.

Robinson, Mary. *You Are a Success!* Portland, Oreg.: Heart Publishing, 1991.

Sashkin, Marshall. *How to Become a Visionary Leader.* Bryn Mawr, Pa.: Organization Design and Development, 1986.

Schuller, Robert H. *Tough Times Never Last, but Tough People Do.* Toronto: Bantam Books, 1983.

Schutz, Will. *The Human Element.* Muir Beach, Calif.: Will Schutz Associates, 1980.

Schutz, Will. *Profound Simplicity.* New York: Bantam Books, 1979.

Sherwood, Keith. *The Art of Spiritual Healing.* St. Paul, Minn.: Llewellyn Publications, 1986.

Smalley, Gary. *Hidden Keys to Loving Relationships.* Paoli, Pa.: Relationships Today (Audiotape), 1988.

Smalley, Gary. *Hidden Keys to Successful Parenting.* Paoli, Pa.: Relationships Today (Audiotape), 1988.

Staw, Barry M. (Ed.). *Psychological Foundations of Organizational Behavior.* Santa Monica, Calif.: Goodyear Publishing, 1977.

Steers, Richard M. *Organizational Effectiveness: A Behavioral View.* Santa Monica, Calif.: Goodyear Publishing, 1977.

Tice, Louis. *Achieving Your Potential.* Seattle: The Pacific Institute, 1976.

Tichy, Noel. "Remaking Your Firm for the 21st Century." *The Sound Management Report,* Vol. 1, No. 2. Chicago: Nightingale-Conant, 1989.

Tracy, Brian. *The Psychology of Achievement.* Chicago: Nightingale-Conant (Audiotape), 1984.

Tracy, Brian. "Putting Your Career on the Fast Track," *The Sound Management Report,* Vol. 1, No. 2. Chicago: Nightingale-Conant, 1989a.

Tracy, Brian. "What Integrity Can Do for Your Business," *The Sound Management Report,* Vol. 1, No. 5. Chicago: Nightingale-Conant, 1989b.

Tulku, Tarthang. *Skillful Means.* Berkeley, Calif.: Dharma Publishing, 1978.

Vance, Mike. *Creative Thinking.* Chicago: Nightingale-Conant (Audiotape), 1982.

Viscott, David. *Building a Magic Relationship.* Albuquerque, N.M.: Newman Communications (Audiotape), 1986.

von Oech, Roger. *A Kick in the Seat of the Pants.* New York: Harper and Row, 1986.

von Oech, Roger. *A Whack on the Side of the Head.* New York: Warner Books, 1983.

Waitley, Denis E. *The Psychology of Winning.* Chicago: Nightingale-Conant (Audiotape), 1988.

Whitfield, Charles L. *Healing the Child Within.* Deerfield Beach, Calif.: Health Communications, 1987.

Wickett, Mike. *It's All Within Your Reach.* Chicago: Nightingale-Conant (Audiotape), 1987.

INDEX

110–112; guidelines for giving, 172–173, 191–192; guidelines for receiving, 187–189, 191–192; inconsistency in patterns of, 192–193; in performance evaluations, 58–59, 114–115, 175–176; positive-to-negative pattern of, 192; positive type of, 191–192; of present-moment experience, 176–179; in relationships, 19–20, 59, 137–138, 186, 193; requests for, 58–59; resistance to, 185–187, 191; reward for, 188–189; and safety, 189–191, 193; and separation of person from problem, 172–176; in straight-talk three-step strategy, 176–179. *See also* Communication
Feelings: communication of, 166–168; denying or burial of, 167–168; in straight-talk three-step strategy, 176–179
Fisher, R., 172, 198, 239
Focus, and head-heart connection, 102–104
Followership, 62
Ford, H., 61
Forgetting, 56–57
Forgiveness, 131–133

Gandhi, M., 237
General Motors, 210–211
Goals, identification of, 231–232
Golden Rule, spirit of, 179–183
Gorbachev, M., 79
Gratification, postponement of, 69
Grinder, J., 137, 140
Growing edge, 109–110
Growth. *See* Change process; Learning; Transformation

Hanley, J., 228
Head-heart connection: and balance, 104–106; and focus, 102–104; importance of, 101–102; and integrity, 243–244; and listening, 200, 202; for organizations, 103–104; and teachers, 248, 251
Hendricks, G., 21, 128, 154, 155, 209, 226
Hendricks, K., 128, 154, 155, 226

Hewitt Associates, 104
Hill, N., 235
Holmes, O. W., 101, 107
Honda of America, 60
Honesty. *See* Truth
Hopper, G., 61
"Horn–halo" effect, 81–82
Hume, D., 60

"I can't/I won't," 61
"I didn't mean to," 63
"I don't care" attitude, 241
"I don't have time," 63
"I don't know," 55–56
"I forgot," 56–57
"I had no choice," 54–55, 79
"I had no control," 55
IBM, 60, 104, 110–111
"If-then" strategy, 57–58
"I'll try," 57
"I'll wait and see," 62
Illiteracy, 254
Incompletes: acceptance of, 134; awareness checks for, 124, 130–131; and body talk, 123–125; breaking the pattern of, 125–131; categories of, 126–128; completion of, 133–134; definition of, 125; exercises on, 125–126, 129–130; and forgiveness, 131–133; impact of, 125, 128; strategies for breaking the pattern of, 129–131
Influencing, 237–239
Influential listening, 197, 198–202. *See also* Listening
Integrity: in adversity, 238–239; awareness checks on, 243; companies with, 239; and head-heart connection, 243–244; influencing with, 237–238; and keeping agreements, 239–243
Intent in listening, 201–202
Intent to communicate, 157, 159–164
Interest, compared with commitment, 229
Internal versus external forces, 42–44
International relations, 54–55, 78–79, 166, 180–181, 195–196, 199, 229, 243
Intuition, 125

Allenbaugh Associates, Inc.

Allenbaugh Associates, Inc., an organization development consulting firm, focuses on seven key areas to enhance both individual and organizational excellence:

1. Shaping corporate culture (vision and values)
2. Enhancing leadership skills
3. Building partnership or teamwork
4. Building a client-focused organization
5. Developing strategic direction and long-range plans
6. Coaching and mentoring top executives
7. Conducting executive and board retreats

Applying the principles explored in this book, Dr. Allenbaugh becomes a catalyst for organizational change emphasizing vision, values, partnership, accountability, and integrity of both products and process. Directed primarily toward service-oriented organizations, this value-driven approach balances the bottom line with the human element. People learn to honor differences while sharing a common vision. They learn to make a positive difference in their own lives while simultaneously serving the corporate mission. And they learn the value of unity over uniformity. The empowered organization achieves enhanced results while getting the "wild ducks to fly in formation."

Dr. Allenbaugh frequently speaks at seminars and conventions on individual and organizational peak performance. For more information about the speaking and consulting services of Allenbaugh Associates, Inc., and soon-to-be-released personal and professional development audiotapes, contact:

G. Eric Allenbaugh, Ph.D., President
Allenbaugh Associates, Inc.
17545 Kelok Road
Lake Oswego, Oregon 97034
503-635-3963

O R D E R   N O W !

Wake-Up Calls:
You Don't Have to Sleepwalk
Through Your Life, Love, or Career!
Cloth Bound Edition $18.95

Quantity Discounts
are available with
multiple copy purchases.

1-800-945-3132